THIRD EDITION

Oracle PL/SQL Language
Pocket Reference

*Steven Feuerstein, Bill Pribyl,
and Chip Dawes*

O'REILLY®

Beijing · Cambridge · Farnham · Köln · Paris · Sebastopol · Taipei · Tokyo

Oracle PL/SQL Language Pocket Reference, Third Edition

by Steven Feuerstein, Bill Pribyl, and Chip Dawes

Copyright © 2004, 2003, 1999 O'Reilly Media, Inc. All rights reserved.
Printed in the United States of America.

Published by O'Reilly Media, Inc., 1005 Gravenstein Highway North,
Sebastopol, CA 95472.

O'Reilly Media, Inc. books may be purchased for educational, business, or
sales promotional use. Online editions are also available for most titles
(*safari.oreilly.com*). For more information, contact our corporate/
institutional sales department: (800) 998-9938 or *corporate@oreilly.com*.

Editor:	Deborah Russell
Production Editor:	Mary Brady
Cover Designer:	Edie Freedman
Interior Designer:	David Futato

Printing History:

April 1999:	First Edition.
February 2003:	Second Edition.
April 2004:	Third Edition.

ISBN-10: 0-596-00680-2
ISBN-13: 978-0-596-00680-8
[C]   [10/06]

Contents

Oracle PL/SQL Language Pocket Reference

Introduction

The *Oracle PL/SQL Language Pocket Reference* is a quick reference guide to the PL/SQL programming language, which provides procedural extensions to the SQL relational database language and a range of Oracle development tools. Where a package, program, or function is supported only for a particular version of Oracle (e.g., Oracle Database 10g), we indicate this in the text.

The purpose of this pocket reference is to help PL/SQL users find the syntax of specific language elements. It is not a self-contained user guide; basic knowledge of the PL/SQL programming language is required. For more information, see the following O'Reilly books:

Oracle PL/SQL Programming, Third Edition, by Steven Feuerstein with Bill Pribyl

Learning Oracle PL/SQL, by Bill Pribyl with Steven Feuerstein

Oracle in a Nutshell, by Rick Greenwald and David C. Kreines

Oracle PL/SQL Best Practices, by Steven Feuerstein

Acknowledgments

Many thanks to all those who helped in the preparation of this book. In particular, thanks to first-edition reviewers Eric J. Givler and Stephen Nelson, to second-edition reviewer Jonathan Gennick, and to both Bryn Llewellyn and Jonathan Gennick for their input on this latest revision. In addition, we appreciate all the good work by the O'Reilly crew in editing and producing this book.

Conventions

UPPERCASE indicates PL/SQL keywords.

lowercase indicates user-defined items such as parameters.

Italic indicates filenames and parameters within text, as well as the first use of a term.

Constant width is used for code examples and output.

Constant width bold indicates user input in examples showing an interaction.

[ ] enclose optional items in syntax descriptions.

{} enclose a list of items in syntax descriptions; you must choose one item from the list.

| separates bracketed list items in syntax descriptions.

PL/SQL Language Fundamentals

This section summarizes the fundamental components of the PL/SQL language: characters, identifiers, literals, delimiters, use of comments and pragmas, and construction of statements and blocks.

PL/SQL Character Set

The PL/SQL language is constructed from letters, digits, symbols, and whitespace, as defined in the following table:

Type	Characters
Letters	A-Z, a-z
Digits	0-9
Symbols	~!@#$%^&*( )_-+=|[ ]{ }:;"'< >,.?/ ^
Whitespace	space, tab, newline, carriage return

Characters are grouped together into four lexical units: identifiers, literals, delimiters, and comments.

Identifiers

Identifiers are names for PL/SQL objects such as constants, variables, exceptions, procedures, cursors, and reserved words. Identifiers have the following characteristics:

- Can be up to 30 characters in length
- Cannot include whitespace (space, tab, carriage return)
- Must start with a letter
- Can include a dollar sign ($), an underscore (_), and a pound sign (#)
- Are not case-sensitive

In addition, you must not use PL/SQL's reserved words as identifiers. For a list of those words, see the "Reserved Words" section at the end of the book.

If you enclose an identifier within double quotes, all but the first of these rules are ignored. For example, the following declaration is valid:

```
DECLARE
   "1 ^abc" VARCHAR2(100);
BEGIN
   IF "1 ^abc" IS NULL THEN ...
END;
```

Boolean, Numeric, and String Literals

Literals are specific values not represented by identifiers. For example, TRUE, 3.14159, 6.63E-34, 'Moby Dick', and NULL are all literals of type Boolean, number, or string. There are no complex datatype literals as their values are internal representations; complex types receive values through direct assignment or via constructors. Unlike the rest of PL/SQL, literals are case-sensitive. To embed single quotes within a string literal, place two single quotes next to each other.

Oracle Database 10*g* allows you to define your own quoting mechanism for string literals in both your SQL and PL/SQL statements. Use the characters q' (q followed by a straight single quote) to designate the programmer-defined delimiter for your string literal. Terminate the literal string with the programmer-defined delimiter followed by a trailing single quote—for example, q'!my string!'. NCHAR and NVARCHAR delimiters are preceded by the letters nq, as in nq'^nchar string^'. This technique can simplify your code when consecutive single quotes appear within a string, such as the literals in a SQL statement. If you define your delimiter with one of the four bracketing characters ([{<, you must use the righthand version of the bracketing character as the closing delimiter. For example, q'[must be closed with]'.

See the following table for examples:

Literal	Actual value
'That''s Entertainment!'	That's Entertainment!
q'#That's Entertainment!#'	That's Entertainment!
'"The Raven"'	"The Raven"
'TZ=''CDT6CST'''	TZ='CDT6CST'
q'$TZ='CDT6CST'$'	TZ='CDT6CST'
q'[TZ='CDT6CST']'	TZ='CDT6CST'
''''	'
'''hello world'''	'hello world'
q'!'hello world'!'	'hello world'

Literal	Actual value
''''''	''
q'[''']'	''
nq'<Price='£10'>'	Price='£10'
nq'-WHERE name LIKE '%ñ%'-'	WHERE name LIKE '%ñ%'

Numeric Literals

You may achieve improvements in runtime performance by making explicit the datatype of numeric literals. You can do so by including or excluding a decimal point, or by using a trailing f or d, as shown in the following table:

Literal	Datatype
3.14159	NUMBER
42	INTEGER
0.0	NUMBER
3.14159f	BINARY_FLOAT (Oracle Database 10*g*)
3.14159d	BINARY_DOUBLE (Oracle Database 10*g*)

Oracle Database 10*g* introduced several special named constants:

    BINARY_FLOAT_NAN (Not a Number)
    BINARY_FLOAT_INFINITY
    BINARY_FLOAT_MAX_NORMAL
    BINARY_FLOAT_MIN_NORMAL
    BINARY_FLOAT_MAX_SUBNORMAL
    BINARY_FLOAT_MIN_SUBNORMAL

as well as the BINARY_DOUBLE_ versions of these constants.

Datetime Interval Literals

The datetime interval datatypes, introduced in Oracle9*i*, represent a chronological interval expressed in terms of either years and months or days, hours, minutes, seconds, and fractional seconds. Literals of these datatypes require the keyword INTERVAL followed by the literal and format string(s). The interval must go from a larger field to a smaller one, so YEAR TO MONTH is valid, but MONTH TO YEAR is not. See the following table for examples:

Literal	Actual value
INTERVAL '1-3' YEAR TO MONTH	1 year and 3 months later
INTERVAL '125-11' YEAR(3) TO MONTH	125 years and 11 months later
INTERVAL '-18' MONTH	18 months earlier
INTERVAL '-48' HOUR	48 hours earlier
INTERVAL '7 23:15' DAY TO MINUTE	7 days, 23 hours, 15 minutes later
INTERVAL '1 12:30:10.2' DAY TO SECOND	1 day, 12 hours, 30 minutes, 10.2 seconds later
INTERVAL '12:30:10.2' HOUR TO SECOND	12 hours, 30 minutes, 10.2 seconds later

Delimiters

Delimiters are symbols with special meaning, such as := (assignment operator), || (concatenation operator), and ; (statement delimiter). The following table lists the PL/SQL delimiters:

Delimiter	Description
;	Terminator (for statements and declarations)
+	Addition operator
-	Subtraction operator
*	Multiplication operator
/	Division operator
**	Exponentiation operator
||	Concatenation operator
:=	Assignment operator
=	Equality operator
<> and ! =	Inequality operators

Delimiter	Description
^= and ~=	Inequality operators
<	"Less-than" operator
<=	"Less-than or equal to" operator
>	"Greater-than" operator
>=	"Greater-than or equal to" operator
(and)	Expression or list delimiters
<< and >>	Label delimiters
,	(Comma) Item separator
'	(Single quote) Literal delimiter
q' and '	Programmer-defined string literal delimiter
nq' and '	Programmer-defined NCHAR string literal delimiter
"	(Double quote) Quoted literal delimiter
:	Host variable indicator
%	Attribute indicator
.	(Period) Component indicator (as in *record.field* or *package. element*)
@	Remote database indicator (database link)
=>	Association operator (named notation)
..	(Two periods) Range operator (used in the FOR loop)
--	Single-line comment indicator
/* and */	Multiline comment delimiters

Comments

Comments are sections of code that exist to aid readability. The compiler ignores them.

A single-line comment begins with a double hyphen (--) and ends with a new line. The compiler ignores all characters between the -- and the new line.

A multiline comment begins with slash asterisk (/*) and ends with asterisk slash (*/). The /* */ comment delimiters also can be used for a single-line comment. The following block demonstrates both kinds of comments:

```
DECLARE
    -- Two dashes comment out only the physical line.
    /* Everything is a comment until the compiler
       encounters the following symbol */
```

You cannot embed multiline comments within a multiline comment, so be careful during development if you comment out portions of code that include comments. The following code demonstrates this issue:

```
DECLARE
    /* Everything is a comment until the compiler
       /* This comment inside another WON'T work!*/
       encounters the following symbol. */

    /* Everything is a comment until the compiler
       -- This comment inside another WILL work!
       encounters the following symbol. */
```

Pragmas

The PRAGMA keyword is used to give instructions to the compiler. There are four types of pragmas in PL/SQL:

EXCEPTION_INIT
    Tells the compiler to associate the specified error number with an identifier that has been declared an EXCEPTION in your current program or an accessible package. See the "Exception Handling" section for more information on this pragma.

RESTRICT_REFERENCES
    Tells the compiler the purity level of a packaged program. The purity level is the degree to which a program does not read/write database tables and/or package variables. See the "Calling PL/SQL Functions in SQL" section for more information on this pragma.

SERIALLY_REUSABLE

Tells the runtime engine that package data should not persist between references. This is used to reduce per-user memory requirements when the package data is needed only for the duration of the call and not for the duration of the session. See the "Packages" section for more information on this pragma.

AUTONOMOUS_TRANSACTION

Tells the compiler that the function, procedure, top-level anonymous PL/SQL block, object method, or database trigger executes in its own transaction space. See the "Database Interaction" section for more information on this pragma.

Statements

A PL/SQL program is composed of one or more logical statements. A *statement* is terminated by a semicolon delimiter. The physical end-of-line marker in a PL/SQL program is ignored by the compiler, except to terminate a single-line comment (initiated by the -- symbol).

Block Structure

Each PL/SQL program is a *block* consisting of a standard set of elements, identified by keywords (see Figure 1). The block determines the scope of declared elements, and how exceptions are handled and propagated. A block can be anonymous or named. Named blocks include functions, procedures, packages, and triggers.

Here is an example of an anonymous block:

```
DECLARE
   today DATE DEFAULT SYSDATE;
BEGIN
   -- Display the date.
   DBMS_OUTPUT.PUT_LINE ('Today is ' || today);
END;
```

Figure 1. The PL/SQL block structure

Here is a named block that performs the same action:

```
CREATE OR REPLACE PROCEDURE show_the_date
IS
    today DATE DEFAULT SYSDATE;
BEGIN
    -- Display the date.
    DBMS_OUTPUT.PUT_LINE ('Today is ' || today);
END show_the_date;
```

The following table summarizes the sections of a PL/SQL block:

Section	Description
Header	Required for named blocks. Specifies the way the program is called by other PL/SQL blocks. Anonymous blocks do not have a header. They start with the DECLARE keyword if there is a declaration section, or with the BEGIN keyword if there are no declarations.
Declaration	Optional; declares variables, cursors, TYPEs, and local programs that are used in the block's execution and exception sections.
Execution	Optional in package and TYPE specifications; contains statements that are executed when the block is run.
Exception	Optional; describes error-handling behavior for exceptions raised in the executable section.

Variables and Program Data

PL/SQL programs normally are used to manipulate database information. You commonly do this by declaring variables and data structures in your programs, and then working with that PL/SQL-specific data.

A *variable* is a named instantiation of a data structure declared in a PL/SQL block (either locally or in a package). Unless you declare a variable as a CONSTANT, its value can be changed at any time in your program.

The following table summarizes the different types of program data:

Type	Description
Scalar	Variables made up of a single value, such as a number, date, or Boolean
Composite	Variables made up of multiple values, such as a record or a collection
Reference	Pointers to values
LOB	Variables containing large object (LOB) locators

Scalar Datatypes

Scalar datatypes divide into four families: number, character, datetime, and Boolean. Subtypes further define a base datatype by restricting the values or size of the base datatype.

Numeric datatypes

Numeric datatypes represent real numbers, integers, and floating-point numbers. They are stored as NUMBER, BINARY_INTEGER, and IEEE floating-point (Oracle Database 10g) storage types.

Decimal numeric datatypes store fixed and floating-point numbers of just about any size. They include the subtypes NUMBER, DEC, DECIMAL, NUMERIC, FLOAT, REAL, and DOUBLE PRECISION. The maximum precision of a variable with type NUMBER is 38 digits, which yields a range of values from 1.0E-129 through 9.999E125.

Variables of type NUMBER can be declared with precision and scale, as follows:

```
NUMBER(precision, scale)
```

where *precision* is the number of digits, and *scale* is the number of digits to the right (positive scale) or left (negative scale) of the decimal point at which rounding occurs. Legal values for *scale* range from -84 to 127. The following table shows examples of *precision* and *scale*:

Declaration	Assigned value	Stored value
NUMBER	6.02	6.02
NUMBER(4)	8675	8675
NUMBER(4)	8675309	Error
NUMBER(12,5)	3.14159265	3.14159
NUMBER(12,-5)	8675309	8700000

Oracle provides a variety of datatypes to store 32-bit whole numbers: BINARY_INTEGER, INTEGER, INT, SMALLINT, NATURAL, NATURALN, POSITIVE, POSITIVEN, SIGN-TYPE, and PLS_INTEGER. Prior to Oracle Database 10g, all of these except PLS_INTEGER were manipulated using the same C-language arithmetic library as the NUMBER datatype. PLS_INTEGER, however, uses machine arithmetic, which is up to three times faster than library arithmetic. In the new release, the distinction among these datatypes has been eliminated, and all of these whole number datatypes now use the speedier machine arithmetic.

Binary integer datatypes store signed integers in the range of $-2^{31} + 1$ to $2^{31} - 1$. The subtypes include NATURAL (0 through 2^{31}) and POSITIVE (1 through 2^{31}) together with the NOT NULL variations NATURALN and POSITIVEN. SIGN-TYPE is restricted to three values (-1, 0, 1). PLS_INTEGER is an unconstrained subtype (alias) of BINARY_INTEGER.

Oracle Database 10g introduced IEEE 754–compliant floating-point numbers to both SQL and PL/SQL. These subtypes are the single-precision BINARY_FLOAT and the double-precision BINARY_DOUBLE. Because these datatypes require less memory and use native machine arithmetic, they perform much better for scientific or engineering applications that are compute-intensive or that require comparison to infinity or Not a Number (NaN). These two datatypes have binary precision instead of the decimal precision used in the NUMBER family. So, if you are developing financial applications that are concerned with rounding errors or require decimal precision, you probably should not use these floating-point datatypes.

The following table lists the PL/SQL numeric datatypes with ANSI and IBM compatibility. In this table:

- *prec* is the precision for the subtype.
- *scale* is the scale of the subtype.
- *binary* is the binary precision of the subtype.

PL/SQL datatype	Compatibility	Oracle RDBMS datatype
DEC(*prec,scale*)	ANSI	NUMBER(*prec,scale*)
DECIMAL(*prec,scale*)	IBM	NUMBER(*prec,scale*)
DOUBLE PRECISION	ANSI	NUMBER
FLOAT(*binary*)	ANSI, IBM	NUMBER
INT	ANSI	NUMBER(38)
INTEGER	ANSI, IBM	NUMBER(38)
NUMERIC(*prec,scale*)	ANSI	NUMBER(*prec,scale*)
REAL	ANSI	NUMBER
SMALLINT	ANSI, IBM	NUMBER(38)
BINARY_FLOAT	IEEE 754	BINARY_FLOAT
BINARY_DOUBLE	IEEE 754	BINARY_DOUBLE

Character datatypes

Character datatypes store alphanumeric text and are manipulated by character functions. As with the numeric family, there are several subtypes in the character family, shown in the following table:

Family	Description
CHAR	Fixed-length alphanumeric strings. Valid sizes are 1 to 32767 bytes (which is larger than the Oracle database limit of 4000).
VARCHAR2	Variable-length alphanumeric strings. Valid sizes are 1 to 32767 bytes (which is larger than the Oracle database limit of 4000).
LONG	Variable-length alphanumeric strings. Valid sizes are 1 to 32760 bytes. LONG is included primarily for backward compatibility. CLOB is the preferred datatype for large character strings.
RAW	Variable-length binary strings. Valid sizes are 1 to 32767 bytes (which is larger than the Oracle database limit of 2000). RAW data does not undergo character set conversion when selected from a remote database.
LONG RAW	Variable-length binary strings. Valid sizes are 1 to 32760 bytes. LONG RAW is included primarily for backward compatibility. BLOB and BFILE are the preferred datatypes for large binary data.
ROWID	Fixed-length binary data. Every row in a database has a physical address or ROWID. A ROWID has four parts in base 64: *OOOOOOFFFBBBBBBBBRRR* where: *OOOOOO* is the object number. *FFFF* is the absolute or relative file number. *BBBBBBBBB* is the block number within the file. *RRRR* is the row number within the block.
UROWID	Universal ROWID. Variable-length hexadecimal string depicting a logical, physical, or non-Oracle row identifier. Valid sizes are up to 4000 bytes.

Datetime datatypes

The datetime datatypes, introduced in Oracle9*i*, are DATE, TIMESTAMP, TIMESTAMP WITH TIME ZONE, and TIMESTAMP WITH LOCAL TIME ZONE. There are also two interval datatypes, INTERVAL YEAR TO MONTH and INTERVAL DAY TO SECOND.

DATE values are fixed-length, date-plus-time values. The DATE datatype can store dates from January 1, 4712 B.C. to December 31, 9999 A.D. Each DATE includes the century, year, month, day, hour, minute, and second. Subsecond granularity is not supported via the DATE datatype; use one of the TIMESTAMP datatypes instead. The time portion of a DATE defaults to midnight (12:00:00 a.m.) if it is not included explicitly.

TIMESTAMP values store date and time to subsecond granularity. The subsecond precision (the number of digits to the right of the decimal) either defaults or is set to 0 through 9 digits by declaration, as in:

```
DECLARE
  mytime_declared TIMESTAMP(9);
  mytime_default  TIMESTAMP;
```

The default precision is 6 digits of precision to the right of the decimal.

TIMESTAMP WITH TIME ZONE values store date and time values like a TIMESTAMP but also store the hourly offset from Coordinated Universal Time (UTC, which is essentially equivalent to Greenwich Mean Time). As with TIMESTAMP, the subsecond precision is 0 to 9 digits, either declared or inherited from the default 6 digits of precision:

```
DECLARE
  mytime_declared TIMESTAMP(9) WITH TIME ZONE;
  mytime_default  TIMESTAMP WITH TIME ZONE;
```

TIMESTAMP WITH LOCAL TIME ZONE values store date and time values together with the UTC offset, like a TIMESTAMP WITH TIME ZONE. The principal difference between these timestamp datatypes occurs when values are saved to or retrieved from a database table. TIMESTAMP WITH LOCAL TIME ZONE values are converted to the database time zone and saved without an offset. The values retrieved from the database table are converted from the database time zone to the session's time zone.

The offset from UTC for both TIMESTAMP WITH TIME ZONE and TIMESTAMP WITH LOCAL TIME ZONE can be hours and minutes or a time zone region (found in the V$TIMEZONE_NAMES data dictionary view) with the optional daylight savings time name (also found in V$TIMEZONE_NAMES). For example:

```
ALTER SESSION SET NLS_TIMESTAMP_TZ_FORMAT=
   'DD-Mon-YYYY HH24:MI:SS.FF TZR';
DECLARE
   my_tswtz      TIMESTAMP(4) WITH TIME ZONE;
BEGIN
   my_tswtz := '31-JUL-02 07:32:45.1234 US/Pacific';
```

INTERVAL YEAR TO MONTH values store a period of time in years and months:

```
DECLARE
   myy2m INTERVAL YEAR TO MONTH;
BEGIN
   myy2m := INTERVAL '1-6' YEAR TO MONTH;
```

INTERVAL DAY TO SECOND values store a period of time in days, hours, minutes, seconds, and fractional seconds:

```
DECLARE
   myd2s INTERVAL DAY TO SECOND;
BEGIN
   myd2s := INTERVAL '2 10:32:15.678' DAY TO SECOND;
```

BOOLEAN datatype

The BOOLEAN datatype can store one of only three values: TRUE, FALSE, or NULL. BOOLEAN variables usually are used in logical control structures such as IF...THEN or LOOP statements.

The following truth tables show the results of logical AND, OR, and NOT operations with PL/SQL's three-value Boolean model:

AND	TRUE	FALSE	NULL
TRUE	TRUE	FALSE	NULL
FALSE	FALSE	FALSE	FALSE
NULL	NULL	FALSE	NULL

OR	TRUE	FALSE	NULL
TRUE	TRUE	TRUE	TRUE
FALSE	TRUE	FALSE	NULL
NULL	TRUE	NULL	NULL

NOT (TRUE)	NOT (FALSE)	NOT (NULL)
FALSE	TRUE	NULL

NLS Character Datatypes

The standard WE8MSWIN1252 or WE8ISO8859P2 character set does not support some languages, such as Chinese and Greek. To support a secondary character set, Oracle allows two character sets in a database—the database character set and the national character set (NLS).

The two NLS datatypes, NCHAR and NVARCHAR2, are used to represent data in the national character set. NCHAR values are fixed-length character data; the maximum length is 32767 bytes. NVARCHAR2 values are variable-length character data; the maximum length also is 32767 bytes.

LOB Datatypes

PL/SQL supports a number of large object (LOB) datatypes, which can store objects of up to four gigabytes of data. Unlike the scalar datatypes, variables declared for LOBs use locators, or pointers to the actual data. LOBs are manipulated in PL/SQL using the built-in package DBMS_LOB. The LOB datatypes are:

BFILE
> File locators pointing to read-only large binary objects in operating system files. With BFILEs, the large objects are outside the database.

BLOB
> LOB locators that point to large binary objects inside the database.

CLOB
> LOB locators that point to large character (alphanumeric) objects inside the database.

NCLOB
> LOB locators that point to large national character set objects inside the database.

Implicit Datatype Conversions

Whenever PL/SQL detects that a datatype conversion is necessary, it attempts to change the values as required to perform the operation. Figure 2 shows what types of implicit conversions PL/SQL can perform. Note that not all values in each datatype can be converted to another datatype. For example, an attempt to convert BINARY_FLOAT_NAN to a number datatype will raise an INVALID NUMBER exception.

NULLs in PL/SQL

PL/SQL represents unknown or inapplicable values as NULL values. Because a NULL is unknown, a NULL is never equal or not equal to anything (including another NULL value). In addition, most functions return a NULL when passed a NULL argument—the notable exceptions are NVL, NVL2, CONCAT, and REPLACE. You cannot check for equality or inequality to NULL; therefore, you must use the IS NULL or IS NOT NULL syntax to check for NULL values.

Here is an example of the IS NULL syntax used to check the value of a variable:

```
BEGIN
   IF myvar IS NULL
   THEN
      ...
```

Declaring Variables

Before you can use a variable, you must first declare it in the declaration section of your PL/SQL block or in a package as

From \ To	BINARY_INTEGER	BINARY_FLOAT	BINARY_DOUBLE	BLOB	CHAR	CLOB	DATE	DATETIME/INTERVAL	LONG	NUMBER	PLS_INTEGER	RAW	UROWID	VARCHAR2
BINARY_INTEGER	NA	•	•		•					•	•			•
BINARY_FLOAT	•	NA	•		•					•	•			•
BINARY_DOUBLE	•	•	NA		•					•	•			•
BLOB				NA								•		
CHAR	•	•	•		NA	•	•	•	•	•	•	•	•	•
CLOB					•	NA								•
DATE					•		NA							•
DATETIME/INTERVAL					•		•	NA	•					•
LONG					•	•		•	NA			•		•
NUMBER	•	•	•		•				•	NA	•			•
PLS_INTEGER	•	•	•		•				•	•	NA			•
RAW				•	•				•			NA		•
UROWID					•								NA	•
VARCHAR2	•	•	•		•	•	•	•	•	•	•	•	•	NA

Figure 2. Implicit conversions attempted by PL/SQL

a global. When you declare a variable, PL/SQL allocates memory for the variable's value and names the storage location so that the value can be retrieved and changed. The syntax for a variable declaration is:

```
variable_name [CONSTANT] datatype [NOT NULL]
    [{ := | DEFAULT } initial_value];
```

Constrained declarations

The datatype in a declaration can be constrained or unconstrained. Constrained datatypes have a size, scale, or precision limit that is less than the unconstrained datatype. For example:

```
total_sales    NUMBER(15,2);  -- Constrained.
emp_id         VARCHAR2(9);   -- Constrained.
company_number NUMBER;        -- Unconstrained.
book_title     VARCHAR2;      -- Not valid.
```

Constrained declarations require less memory than unconstrained declarations. Not all datatypes can be specified as unconstrained. You cannot, for example, declare a variable to be of type VARCHAR2. You must always specify the maximum size of a variable-length string.

Constants

The CONSTANT keyword in a declaration requires an initial value and does not allow that value to be changed. For example:

```
min_order_qty   NUMBER(1) CONSTANT := 5;
```

Default values

Whenever you declare a variable, it is assigned a default value of NULL. Initializing all variables is distinctive to PL/SQL; in this way, PL/SQL differs from languages such as C and Ada. If you want to initialize a variable to a value other than NULL, you do so in the declaration with either the assignment operator (:=) or the DEFAULT keyword:

```
counter    BINARY_INTEGER := 0;
priority   VARCHAR2(8)    DEFAULT 'LOW';
```

A NOT NULL constraint can be appended to the variable's datatype declaration to indicate that NULL is not a valid value. If you add the NOT NULL constraint, you must explicitly assign an initial value for that variable.

Anchored Declarations

Use the %TYPE attribute to *anchor* the datatype of a scalar variable to either another variable or to a column in a database table or view. Use %ROWTYPE to anchor a record's declaration to a cursor or table (see the "Records in PL/SQL" section for more details on the %ROWTYPE attribute).

The following block shows several variations of anchored declarations:

```
DECLARE
    tot_sales NUMBER(20,2);
    -- Anchor to a PL/SQL variable.
    monthly_sales tot_sales%TYPE;

    -- Anchor to a database column.
    v_ename employee.last_name%TYPE;

    CURSOR mycur IS
       SELECT * FROM employee;

    -- Anchor to a cursor.
    myrec mycur%ROWTYPE;
```

The NOT NULL clause on a variable declaration (but not on a database column definition) follows the %TYPE anchoring and requires anchored declarations to have a default in their declaration. The default value for an anchored declaration can be different from that for the base declaration:

```
tot_sales     NUMBER(20,2) NOT NULL DEFAULT 0;
monthly_sales tot_sales%TYPE DEFAULT 10;
```

Programmer-Defined Subtypes

PL/SQL allows you to define unconstrained scalar subtypes. An unconstrained subtype provides an alias to the original underlying datatype; for example:

```
CREATE OR REPLACE PACKAGE std_types
IS
    -- Declare standard types as globals.
    SUBTYPE dollar_amt_t IS NUMBER;
END std_types;

CREATE OR REPLACE PROCEDURE process_money
IS
    -- Use the global type declared above.
    credit std_types.dollar_amt_t;
    ...
```

A constrained subtype limits or constrains the new datatype to a subset of the original datatype. For example, POSITIVE is a constrained subtype of BINARY_INTEGER. The declaration for POSITIVE in the STANDARD package is:

```
SUBTYPE POSITIVE IS BINARY_INTEGER RANGE 1..2147483647;
```

You can define your own constrained subtypes in your programs:

```
PACKAGE std_types
IS
    SUBTYPE currency_t IS NUMBER (15, 2);

END;
```

Conditional and Sequential Control

PL/SQL includes conditional (IF, CASE) structures as well as sequential control (GOTO, NULL) constructs.

Conditional Control Statements

There are several varieties of IF-THEN-ELSE and CASE structures.

IF-THEN combination

```
IF condition THEN
   executable statement(s)
END IF;
```

For example:

```
IF caller_type = 'VIP' THEN
   generate_response('GOLD');
END IF;
```

IF-THEN-ELSE combination

```
IF condition THEN
   TRUE sequence_of_executable_statement(s)
ELSE
   FALSE/NULL sequence_of_executable_statement(s)
END IF;
```

For example:

```
IF caller_type = 'VIP' THEN
   generate_response('GOLD');
ELSE
   generate_response('BRONZE');
END IF;
```

IF-THEN-ELSIF combination

```
IF condition-1 THEN
   statements-1
ELSIF condition-N THEN
  statements-N
[ELSE
   ELSE statements]
END IF;
```

For example:

```
IF caller_type = 'VIP' THEN
   generate_response('GOLD');
ELSIF priority_client THEN
   generate_response('SILVER');
ELSE
   generate_response('BRONZE');
END IF;
```

CASE statement

CASE statements were introduced in Oracle9i. There are two types of CASE statements: simple and searched.

A simple CASE statement is similar to an IF-THEN-ELSIF structure. The statement has a switch expression immediately after the keyword CASE. The expression is evaluated and compared to the value in each WHEN clause. The first WHEN clause with a matching value is executed and then control passes to the next statement following the END CASE. For example:

```
CASE region_id
   WHEN 'NE' THEN
      mgr_name := 'MINER';
   WHEN 'SE' THEN
      mgr_name := 'KOOI';
   ELSE mgr_name := 'LANE';
END CASE;
```

If a switch expression evaluates to NULL, the ELSE case is the only one that can possibly match; WHEN NULL will never match because Oracle performs an equality comparison on the expressions.

Both the CASE statement and the CASE expression (see the next section) should include an ELSE clause that will execute statements if no WHEN clause evaluates to TRUE because PL/SQL's runtime engine will raise an exception if it finds no matching expression.

The searched CASE statement does not have a switch; instead, each WHEN clause has a complete Boolean expression. The first matching WHEN clause is executed, and control passes to the next statement following the END CASE. For example:

```
CASE
   WHEN region_id = 'EAME' THEN
      mgr_name := 'SCHMIDT';
   WHEN division = 'SALES' THEN
      mgr_name := 'KENNEDY';
   ELSE mgr_name := 'GUPTA';
END CASE;
```

CASE expression

There are also two types of CASE expressions: simple and searched. You can use CASE expressions anywhere that expressions are valid in your SQL or PL/SQL programs.

A simple CASE expression lets you choose an expression to evaluate based on a scalar value that you provide as input. The following example shows a simple CASE expression being used with the built-in DBMS_OUTPUT package to output the value of a Boolean variable. DBMS_OUTPUT.PUT_LINE is not overloaded to handle Boolean types, so in this example the CASE expression converts the Boolean value in a character string, which PUT_LINE can then handle:

```
DECLARE
    boolean_true BOOLEAN := TRUE;
    boolean_false BOOLEAN := FALSE;
    boolean_null BOOLEAN;

    FUNCTION boolean_to_varchar2 (flag IN BOOLEAN)
        RETURN VARCHAR2 IS
    BEGIN
        RETURN
            CASE flag
                WHEN TRUE THEN 'True'
                WHEN FALSE THEN 'False'
                ELSE 'NULL'
        END;
    END;

BEGIN
    DBMS_OUTPUT.PUT_LINE(boolean_to_varchar2(boolean_true));
    DBMS_OUTPUT.PUT_LINE(boolean_to_varchar2(boolean_false));
    DBMS_OUTPUT.PUT_LINE(boolean_to_varchar2(boolean_null));
END;
```

A searched CASE expression evaluates a list of expressions to find the first one that evaluates to TRUE, and then returns the results of an associated expression. In the following example, a searched CASE expression returns the proper bonus value for any given salary:

```
DECLARE
    salary NUMBER := 20000;
    employee_id NUMBER := 36325;
```

```
PROCEDURE give_bonus
  (emp_id IN NUMBER, bonus_amt IN NUMBER) IS
BEGIN
  DBMS_OUTPUT.PUT_LINE(emp_id);
  DBMS_OUTPUT.PUT_LINE(bonus_amt);
END;

BEGIN
  give_bonus(employee_id,
    CASE
      WHEN salary >= 10000 AND salary <=20000 THEN 1500
      WHEN salary > 20000 AND salary <= 40000 THEN 1000
      WHEN salary > 40000 THEN 500
      ELSE 0
    END);
END;
```

Sequential Control Statements

PL/SQL provides a GOTO statement and a NULL statement to aid in sequential control operations.

GOTO

The GOTO statement performs unconditional branching to a named label. You should only rarely use a GOTO. At least one executable statement must follow the label (the NULL statement can be this necessary executable statement). The format of a GOTO statement is:

```
GOTO <<label_name>>;
```

For example:

```
BEGIN
  GOTO second_output;

  DBMS_OUTPUT.PUT_LINE('This line will never execute.');

  <<second_output>>
  DBMS_OUPUT.PUT_LINE('We are here!');
END
```

There are several scope restrictions on where a GOTO can branch control. A GOTO:

- Can branch out of an IF statement, LOOP, or subblock
- Cannot branch into an IF statement, LOOP, or subblock
- Cannot branch from one section of an IF statement to another (from the IF-THEN section to the ELSE section is illegal)
- Cannot branch into or out of a subprogram
- Cannot branch from the exception section to the executable section of a PL/SQL block
- Cannot branch from the executable section to the exception section of a PL/SQL block, although a RAISE does this

NULL

The NULL statement is an executable statement that does nothing. It is useful when an executable statement must follow a GOTO label or to aid readability in an IF-THEN-ELSE structure. For example:

```
IF :report.selection = 'DETAIL' THEN
    exec_detail_report;
ELSE
    NULL;
END IF;
```

Loops

The LOOP construct allows you to execute a sequence of statements repeatedly. There are three types of loops: simple (infinite), FOR, and WHILE.

You can use the EXIT statement to break out of the LOOP and pass control to the statement following the END LOOP.

Simple Loop

```
LOOP
    executable_statement(s)
END LOOP;
```

The simple loop should contain an EXIT or EXIT WHEN unless you want it to execute infinitely. Use the simple loop when you want the body of the loop to execute at least once. For example:

```
LOOP
   FETCH company_cur INTO company_rec;
   EXIT WHEN company_cur%ROWCOUNT > 5 OR
      company_cur%NOTFOUND;
   process_company(company_cur);
END LOOP;
```

Numeric FOR Loop

```
FOR loop_index IN [REVERSE] lowest_number..highest_number
LOOP
   executable_statement(s)
END LOOP;
```

The PL/SQL runtime engine automatically declares the loop index a PLS_INTEGER variable; never declare a variable with that name yourself. The *lowest_number* and *highest_number* ranges can be variables, but are evaluated only once—on initial entry into the loop. The REVERSE keyword causes PL/SQL to start with the *highest_number* and decrement down to the *lowest_number*. For example, this code:

```
BEGIN
   FOR counter IN 1 .. 4
   LOOP
      DBMS_OUTPUT.PUT(counter);
   END LOOP;
   DBMS_OUTPUT.NEW_LINE;

   FOR counter IN REVERSE 1 .. 4
   LOOP
      DBMS_OUTPUT.PUT(counter);
   END LOOP;
   DBMS_OUTPUT.NEW_LINE;
END;
```

yields the following output:

```
1234
4321
```

Cursor FOR Loop

```
FOR record_index IN [cursor_name | (SELECT statement)]
LOOP
   executable_statement(s)
END LOOP;
```

The PL/SQL runtime engine automatically declares the loop index a record of *cursor_name*%ROWTYPE; never declare a variable with that name yourself.

The cursor FOR loop automatically opens the cursor, fetches all rows identified by the cursor, and then closes the cursor. You can embed the SELECT statement directly in the cursor FOR loop. For example:

```
FOR emp_rec IN emp_cur
LOOP
   IF emp_rec.title = 'Oracle Programmer'
   THEN
      give_raise(emp_rec.emp_id,30)
   END IF;
END LOOP;
```

WHILE Loop

```
WHILE condition
LOOP
   executable_statement(s)
END LOOP;
```

Use the WHILE loop in cases where you may not want the loop body to execute even once:

```
WHILE NOT end_of_analysis
LOOP
   perform_analysis;
   get_next_record;
   IF analysis_cursor%NOTFOUND AND next_step IS NULL
   THEN
      end_of_analysis := TRUE;
   END IF;
END LOOP;
```

REPEAT UNTIL Loop Emulation

PL/SQL does not directly support a REPEAT UNTIL construct, but a modified simple loop can emulate one. The syntax for this emulated REPEAT UNTIL loop is:

```
LOOP
    executable_statement(s)
    EXIT WHEN Boolean_condition;
END LOOP;
```

Use the emulated REPEAT UNTIL loop when executing iterations indefinitely before conditionally terminating the loop.

EXIT Statement

```
EXIT [WHEN condition];
```

If you do not include a WHEN clause in the EXIT statement, it will terminate the loop unconditionally. Otherwise, the loop terminates only if the Boolean *condition* evaluates to TRUE. The EXIT statement is optional and can appear anywhere in the loop.

Loop Labels

Loops can be optionally labeled to improve readability and execution control, as we showed earlier in the discussion of the GOTO statement. The label must appear immediately in front of the statement that initiates the loop.

The following example demonstrates the use of loop labels to qualify variables within a loop and also to terminate nested and outer loops:

```
<<year_loop>>
FOR yearind IN 1 .. 20
LOOP
    <<month_loop>>
    LOOP
        ...
        IF year_loop.yearind > 10
        THEN
```

```
            EXIT year_loop;
        END IF;
    END LOOP month_loop;
END LOOP year_loop;
```

Database Interaction

PL/SQL is tightly integrated with the underlying SQL layer of the Oracle database. You can execute SQL statements (UPDATE, INSERT, DELETE, MERGE, and SELECT) directly in PL/SQL programs. You also can execute Data Definition Language (DDL) statements through the use of dynamic SQL. In addition, you can manage transactions with COMMIT, ROLLBACK, and other Data Control Language (DCL) statements.

Transaction Management

The Oracle RDBMS provides a transaction model based on a unit of work. The PL/SQL language supports most, but not all, of the database model for transactions (you cannot, for example, specify ROLLBACK FORCE). A transaction begins with the first change to data and ends with either a COMMIT or a ROLLBACK. Transactions are independent of PL/SQL blocks. Transactions can span multiple PL/SQL blocks, or multiple transactions can be in a single PL/SQL block. The PL/SQL-supported transaction statements include COMMIT, ROLLBACK, SAVEPOINT, SET TRANSACTION, and LOCK TABLE, described in the following sections.

COMMIT

```
COMMIT [WORK] [COMMENT text];
```

COMMIT makes the database changes permanent and visible to other database sessions. The WORK keyword is optional and only aids readability—it is rarely used. The COMMENT text is optional and can be up to 50 characters in length. It is germane only to in-doubt distributed (two-phase commit) transactions. The database statement COMMIT FORCE, also for distributed transactions, is not supported in PL/SQL.

ROLLBACK

```
ROLLBACK [WORK] [TO [SAVEPOINT] savepoint_name];
```

ROLLBACK undoes the changes made in the current transaction either to the beginning of the transaction or to a *savepoint*. A savepoint is a named processing point in a transaction, created with the SAVEPOINT statement. Rolling back to a savepoint is a partial rollback of a transaction, wiping out all changes (and savepoints) that occurred later than the named savepoint.

SAVEPOINT

```
SAVEPOINT savepoint_name;
```

SAVEPOINT establishes a savepoint in the current transaction. *savepoint_name* is an undeclared identifier. More than one savepoint can be established within a transaction. If you reuse a savepoint name, that savepoint is moved to the later position and you will not be able to roll back to the initial savepoint position.

SET TRANSACTION

```
SET TRANSACTION READ ONLY;
SET TRANSACTION ISOLATION LEVEL SERIALIZABLE;
SET TRANSACTION USE ROLLBACK SEGMENT rbseg_name;
```

SET TRANSACTION has three transaction control functions:

READ ONLY
Marks the beginning of a read-only transaction. This indicates to the RDBMS that a read-consistent view of the database is to be enforced for the transaction (the default is for the statement). This read-consistent view means that only changes committed before the transaction begins are visible for the duration of the transaction.

The transaction is ended with either a COMMIT or a ROLLBACK. Only LOCK TABLE, SELECT, SELECT INTO, OPEN, FETCH, CLOSE, COMMIT, and ROLLBACK statements are permitted during a read-only transaction. Issuing other statements, such as INSERT or UPDATE, in a read-only transaction results in an ORA-1456 error.

ISOLATION LEVEL SERIALIZABLE

Similar to a READ ONLY transaction in that transaction-level read consistency is enforced rather than the default statement-level read consistency. Serializable transactions do allow changes to data, however.

USE ROLLBACK SEGMENT

Tells the RDBMS to use the specifically named rollback segment *rbseg_name*. This statement is useful when only one rollback segment is large, and a program knows that it needs to use the large rollback segment, such as during a month-end close operation. For example, if we know that our large rollback segment is named rbs_large, we can tell the database to use it by issuing the following statement before our first change to data:

```
SET TRANSACTION USE ROLLBACK SEGMENT rbs_large;
```

LOCK TABLE

```
LOCK TABLE table_list IN lock_mode MODE [NOWAIT];
```

This statement bypasses the implicit database row-level locks by explicitly locking one or more tables in the specified mode. The *table_list* is a comma-delimited list of tables. The *lock_mode* is one of the following: ROW SHARE, ROW EXCLUSIVE, SHARE UPDATE, SHARE, SHARE ROW EXCLUSIVE, or EXCLUSIVE. The NOWAIT keyword specifies that the RDBMS should not wait for a lock to be released. If there is a lock when NOWAIT is specified, the RDBMS raises the exception "ORA-00054: resource busy and acquire with NOWAIT specified." The default RDBMS locking behavior is to wait indefinitely.

Autonomous Transactions

Autonomous transactions execute within a block of code as separate transactions from the outer (main) transaction. Changes can be committed or rolled back in an autonomous transaction without committing or rolling back the main transaction. Changes committed in an autonomous transaction are visible to the main transaction, even though they occur after the start of the main transaction. Those changes committed in an autonomous transaction are visible to other transactions as well. The RDBMS suspends the main transaction while the autonomous transaction executes:

```
PROCEDURE main IS
BEGIN
   UPDATE ... -- Main transaction begins here.
   DELETE ...
   at_proc;   -- Call the autonomous transaction.
   SELECT ...
   INSERT ...
   COMMIT;    -- Main transaction ends here.
END;

PROCEDURE at_proc IS
   PRAGMA AUTONOMOUS_TRANSACTION;
BEGIN          -- Main transaction suspends here.
   SELECT ...
   INSERT ... -- Autonomous transaction begins here.
   UPDATE ...
   DELETE ...
   COMMIT;    -- Autonomous transaction ends here.
END;           -- Main transaction resumes here.
```

So, changes made in the main transaction are not visible to the autonomous transaction, and if the main transaction holds any locks that the autonomous transaction waits for, a deadlock occurs. Using the NOWAIT option on UPDATE statements in autonomous transactions can help to minimize this kind of deadlock. Functions and procedures (local program, standalone, or packaged), database triggers, top-level anonymous PL/SQL blocks, and object methods can be declared autonomous via the compiler directive PRAGMA

AUTONOMOUS_TRANSACTION. In addition, there must be a COMMIT or a ROLLBACK at each exit point in the autonomous program.

Cursors in PL/SQL

Every SQL statement executed by the RDBMS has a private SQL area that contains information about the SQL statement and the set of data returned. In PL/SQL, a *cursor* is a name assigned to a specific private SQL area for a specific SQL statement. There can be either static cursors, whose SQL statement is determined at compile time, or dynamic cursors, whose SQL statement is determined at runtime. Static cursors are used only for Data Manipulation Language (DML) statements (SELECT, INSERT, UPDATE, DELETE, MERGE, or SELECT FOR UPDATE). These static cursors may be explicitly declared and named or may appear inline as implicit cursors. Dynamic cursors are used for any type of valid SQL statement including DDL (CREATE, TRUN-CATE, ALTER) and DCL (GRANT, REVOKE). Dynamic cursors are implemented with the EXECUTE IMMEDIATE statement.

Explicit Cursors

Explicit cursors are SELECT statements that are DECLAREd explicitly in the declaration section of the current block or in a package specification. Use OPEN, FETCH, and CLOSE in the execution or exception sections of your programs.

Declaring explicit cursors

To use an explicit cursor, you must first declare it in the declaration section of a block or package. There are three types of explicit cursor declarations:

- A cursor without parameters; for example:

```
CURSOR company_cur
   IS
   SELECT company_id FROM company;
```

- A cursor that accepts arguments through a parameter list; for example:

```
CURSOR company_cur (id_in IN NUMBER)
   IS
   SELECT name FROM company
    WHERE  company_id = id_in;
```

- A cursor header that contains a RETURN clause in place of the SELECT statement; for example:

```
CURSOR company_cur (id_in IN NUMBER)
RETURN company%ROWTYPE;
```

This last example shows that the cursor can be declared separately from its implementation: for example, the header in a package specification and the implementation in the package body. See the "Packages" section for more information.

Opening explicit cursors

To open a cursor, use the following syntax:

```
OPEN cursor_name [(argument [,argument ...])];
```

where *cursor_name* is the name of the cursor as declared in the declaration section. The arguments are required if the definition of the cursor contains a parameter list.

You must open an explicit cursor before you can fetch rows from that cursor. When the cursor is opened, the processing actually includes the parse, bind, open, and execute phases of SQL statement execution. This OPEN processing includes determining an execution plan, associating host variables and cursor parameters with the placeholders in the SQL statement, determining the result set, and, finally, setting the current row pointer to the first row in the result set.

When using a cursor FOR loop, the OPEN is implicit in the FOR statement. If you try to open a cursor that is already open, PL/SQL will raise an "ORA-06511: PL/SQL: cursor already open" exception.

Fetching from explicit cursors

The FETCH statement places the contents of the current row into local variables. To retrieve all rows in a result set, each row needs to be fetched. The syntax for a FETCH statement is:

```
FETCH cursor_name INTO record_or_variable_list;
```

where *cursor_name* is the name of the cursor as declared and opened.

Closing explicit cursors

After all rows have been fetched, a cursor needs to be closed. Closing a cursor enables the PL/SQL memory optimization algorithm to release the associated memory at an appropriate time. You can close an explicit cursor by specifying a CLOSE statement as follows:

```
CLOSE cursor_name;
```

where *cursor_name* is the name of the cursor declared and opened.

If you declare a cursor in a local anonymous, procedure, or function block, that cursor will close automatically when the block terminates. Package-based cursors must be closed explicitly, or they stay open for the duration of your session. Closing a cursor that is not open raises an INVALID_CURSOR exception.

Explicit cursor attributes

There are four attributes associated with cursors: ISOPEN, FOUND, NOTFOUND, and ROWCOUNT. These attributes can be accessed with the % delimiter to obtain information about the state of the cursor. The syntax for a cursor attribute is:

```
cursor_name%attribute
```

where *cursor_name* is the name of the explicit cursor.

The behaviors of the explicit cursor attributes are described in the following table:

Attribute	Description
%ISOPEN	TRUE if cursor is open. FALSE if cursor is not open.
%FOUND	INVALID_CURSOR is raised if cursor has not been OPENed. NULL before the first fetch. TRUE if record was fetched successfully. FALSE if no row was returned. INVALID_CURSOR if cursor has been CLOSEd.
%NOTFOUND	INVALID_CURSOR is raised if cursor has not been OPENed. NULL before the first fetch. FALSE if record was fetched successfully. TRUE if no row was returned. INVALID_CURSOR if cursor has been CLOSEd.
%ROWCOUNT	INVALID_CURSOR is raised if cursor has not been OPENed. The number of rows fetched from the cursor. INVALID_CURSOR if cursor has been CLOSEd.

Frequently, a cursor attribute is checked as part of a WHILE loop that fetches rows from a cursor, as shown here:

```
DECLARE
    caller_rec caller_pkg.caller_cur%ROWTYPE;
BEGIN
    OPEN caller_pkg.caller_cur;
    LOOP
        FETCH caller_pkg.caller_cur into caller_rec;
        EXIT WHEN caller_pkg.caller_cur%NOTFOUND
                  OR
                  caller_pkg.caller_cur%ROWCOUNT > 10;

        UPDATE call
            SET caller_id = caller_rec.caller_id
            WHERE call_timestamp < SYSDATE;
    END LOOP;
    CLOSE caller_pkg.caller_cur;
END;
```

Implicit Cursors

Whenever a SQL statement is directly in the execution or exception section of a PL/SQL block, you are working with implicit cursors. SQL statements handled this way include INSERT, UPDATE, DELETE, MERGE, and SELECT INTO. Unlike explicit cursors, implicit cursors do not need to be declared, OPENed, FETCHed, or CLOSEd.

SELECT statements handle the %FOUND and %NOT-FOUND attributes differently from the way that explicit cursors do. When an implicit SELECT statement does not return any rows, PL/SQL immediately raises the NO_DATA_FOUND exception and control passes to the exception section. When an implicit SELECT returns more than one row, PL/SQL immediately raises the TOO_MANY_ROWS exception and control passes to the exception section.

Implicit cursor attributes are referenced via the SQL cursor. For example:

```
BEGIN
   UPDATE activity SET last_accessed := SYSDATE
   WHERE UID = user_id;

   IF SQL%NOTFOUND THEN
      INSERT INTO activity_log (uid,last_accessed)
      VALUES (user_id,SYSDATE);
   END IF
END;
```

The following table lists the implicit cursor attributes:

Attributes	Description
SQL%ISOPEN	Always FALSE because the cursor is opened implicitly and closed immediately after the statement is executed.
SQL%FOUND	NULL before the statement. TRUE if one or more rows were inserted, merged, updated, or deleted, or if only one row was selected. FALSE if no row was selected, merged, updated, inserted, or deleted.

Attributes	Description
SQL%NOTFOUND	NULL before the statement. TRUE if no row was selected, merged, updated, inserted, or deleted. FALSE if one or more rows were inserted, merged, updated, or deleted.
SQL%ROWCOUNT	Number of rows affected by the cursor.
SQL%BULK_ ROWCOUNT	Pseudo index-by table containing the number of rows affected by the statements executed in bulk bind operations. See the "Bulk Binds" section for more information.

Use the RETURNING clause in INSERT, UPDATE, and DELETE statements to obtain data modified by the associated DML statement. This clause allows you to avoid an additional SELECT statement to query the results of the DML statement. For example:

```
BEGIN
   UPDATE activity SET last_accessed := SYSDATE
   WHERE UID = user_id
   RETURNING last_accessed, cost_center
   INTO timestamp, chargeback_acct;
```

SELECT FOR UPDATE clause

By default, the Oracle RDBMS locks rows as they are changed. To lock all rows in a result set, use the FOR UPDATE clause in your SELECT statement when you OPEN the cursor, instead of when you change the data. Using the FOR UPDATE clause does not require you to actually make changes to the data; it only locks the rows when opening the cursor. These locks are released on the next COMMIT or ROLLBACK. As always, these row locks do not affect other SELECT statements unless they, too, are FOR UPDATE. The FOR UPDATE clause is appended to the end of the SELECT statement and has the following syntax:

```
SELECT ...
   FROM ...
      FOR UPDATE [OF column_reference] [NOWAIT];
```

where *column_reference* is a comma-delimited list of columns that appear in the SELECT clause. The NOWAIT keyword tells the RDBMS to not wait for other blocking locks to be released. The default is to wait forever.

In the following example, only columns from the inventory (pet) table are referenced FOR UPDATE, so no rows in the dog_breeds (dog) table are locked when hounds_in_stock_cur is opened:

```
DECLARE
    CURSOR hounds_in_stock_cur IS
        SELECT pet.stock_no, pet.breeder, dog.size
          FROM dog_breeds dog, inventory pet
         WHERE dog.breed = pet.breed
           AND dog.class = 'HOUND'
            FOR UPDATE OF pet.stock_no, pet.breeder;
BEGIN
```

WHERE CURRENT OF clause

UPDATE and DELETE statements can use a WHERE CURRENT OF clause if they reference a cursor declared FOR UPDATE. This syntax indicates that the UPDATE or DELETE should modify the current row identified by the FOR UPDATE cursor. The syntax is:

```
[UPDATE | DELETE ] ...
    WHERE CURRENT OF cursor_name;
```

By using WHERE CURRENT OF, you do not have to repeat the WHERE clause in the SELECT statement. For example:

```
DECLARE
    CURSOR wip_cur IS
        SELECT acct_no, enter_date FROM wip
         WHERE enter_date < SYSDATE - 7
            FOR UPDATE;
BEGIN
    FOR wip_rec IN wip_cur
    LOOP
        INSERT INTO acct_log (acct_no, order_date)
            VALUES (wip_rec.acct_no, wip_rec.enter_date);
        DELETE FROM wip
            WHERE CURRENT OF wip_cur;
    END LOOP;
END;
```

Dynamic Cursors

Dynamic cursors are implemented with an EXECUTE IMME-
DIATE statement together with the OPEN FOR, FETCH, and
CLOSE statements. The EXECUTE IMMEDIATE statement
supports single-row queries and DDL, while the OPEN FOR,
FETCH, and CLOSE statements support dynamic multirow
queries. Here is syntax for these statements:

```
EXECUTE IMMEDIATE sql_statement
   [INTO {variable [,variable ...] | record}]
   [USING [IN | OUT | IN OUT] bind_argument
      [,[IN | OUT | IN OUT] bind_argument ...] ]
   [{RETURNING | RETURN} INTO bind_argument
      [,bind_argument]...];
```

The EXECUTE IMMEDIATE statement parses and executes
the SQL statement in a single step. The EXECUTE IMMEDI-
ATE statement requires a terminating semicolon, but the *sql_
statement* must not have a trailing semicolon. For example:

```
EXECUTE IMMEDIATE 'TRUNCATE TABLE foo';
EXECUTE IMMEDIATE 'GRANT SELECT ON '|| tabname_v ||
   ' TO ' || grantee_list;
```

The OPEN FOR statement assigns a multirow query to a
weakly typed cursor variable. The rows are then FETCHed
and the cursor CLOSEd:

```
DECLARE
   TYPE cv_typ IS REF CURSOR;
   cv cv_typ;
   laccount_no NUMBER;
   lbalance NUMBER;
BEGIN
   OPEN cv FOR
      'SELECT account_no, balance
         FROM accounts
        WHERE balance < 500';
   LOOP
      FETCH cv INTO laccount_no, lbalance;
      EXIT WHEN cv%NOTFOUND;
      -- Process the row.
   END LOOP;
   CLOSE cv;
END;
```

Because SQL statements usually execute repeatedly, declare your dynamic cursor with bind variables and pass the values to Oracle at runtime. The parsed form of the statement can be reused from the shared pool, improving performance. For example:

```
EXECUTE IMMEDIATE 'INSERT INTO hr.regions
  (region_id, region_name) VALUES (:r_id, :r_name)'
  USING  id, name;
```

Cursor Variables

A *cursor variable* is a data structure that points to a cursor object, which in turn points to the cursor's result set. You can use cursor variables to more easily retrieve rows in a result set from client and server programs. You also can use cursor variables to hide minor variations in queries.

The syntax for a REF_CURSOR type (cursor variable) is:

```
TYPE ref_cursor_name IS REF CURSOR
  [RETURN record_type];
```

If you do not include a RETURN clause, you are declaring a "weak" REF CURSOR. Cursor variables declared from weak REF CURSORs can be associated with any query at runtime. A REF CURSOR declaration with a RETURN clause defines a "strong" REF CURSOR. A cursor variable based on a strong REF CURSOR can be associated with queries whose result sets match the number and datatype of the record structure after the RETURN at runtime.

To use cursor variables, you must first create a REF_CURSOR type, then declare a cursor variable based on that type.

The following example shows the use of both weak and strong REF CURSORs:

```
DECLARE
  -- Create a cursor type based on the company table.
  TYPE company_curtype IS REF CURSOR
    RETURN companies%ROWTYPE;
```

```
-- Create the variable based on the REF CURSOR.
company_cur company_curtype;

-- And now the weak, general approach.
TYPE any_curtype IS REF CURSOR;
generic_curvar any_curtype;
```

The syntax to OPEN a cursor variable is:

```
OPEN cursor_name FOR SELECT_statement;
```

FETCH and CLOSE a cursor variable using the same syntax as for explicit cursors. There are several restrictions on cursor variables:

- You cannot declare package-level cursor variables because they do not have a persistent state. (You can declare them in packaged procedures and functions, however.)

- You cannot assign NULLs to a cursor variable nor can you use comparison operators to test for equality, inequality, or nullity.

- Neither database columns nor collections can store cursor variables.

- You cannot use RPCs to pass cursor variables from one server to another.

Cursor Expressions

A *cursor expression* is a cursor that is used as a column expression in the SELECT list of an explicit cursor. The syntax for a cursor expression is:

```
CURSOR (subquery)
```

Cursor expressions can reduce the amount of redundant data returned to a calling program over techniques that involve joining the tables together. The cursor expression is opened automatically when the parent row is fetched. Cursor expressions can be nested as well. These nested cursors are closed when one of the following occurs:

- The nested cursor is explicitly closed by the program.
- The parent cursor is closed.
- The parent cursor is reexecuted.
- An exception is raised during the fetch of the parent row.

An example of a cursor expression follows:

```
DECLARE
   TYPE refcursor IS REF CURSOR;
   CURSOR order_cur IS
      SELECT o.order_date ,o.order_status
         ,CURSOR(SELECT p.translated_name
                        ,i.unit_price
                        ,i.quantity
                   FROM oe.order_items i
                        ,oe.product_descriptions p
                   WHERE i.product_id = p.product_id
                   AND   i.order_id = o.order_id)
      FROM oe.orders o
      WHERE order_date BETWEEN TO_DATE('01-Jan-03')
                        AND TO_DATE('31-Jan-03');
   odate   oe.orders.order_date%TYPE;
   ostatus oe.orders.order_status%TYPE;
   od_cur  refcursor;
   tname   oe.product_descriptions.translated_name%TYPE;
   price   oe.order_items.unit_price%TYPE;
   qty     oe.order_items.quantity%TYPE;
BEGIN
   OPEN order_cur;
   LOOP
      FETCH order_cur INTO odate, ostatus, od_cur;
      EXIT WHEN order_cur%NOTFOUND;
      LOOP
         FETCH od_cur INTO tname, price, qty;
         EXIT WHEN od_cur%NOTFOUND;
         DBMS_OUTPUT.PUT_LINE(odate||','||ostatus
            ||','||tname||','||price||','||qty);
      END LOOP;
   END LOOP;
   CLOSE order_cur;
END;
```

Exception Handling

PL/SQL allows developers to raise and handle errors (exceptions) in a very flexible and powerful way. Each PL/SQL block can have its own exception section in which exceptions can be trapped and handled (resolved or passed on to the enclosing block).

When an exception occurs (is raised) in a PL/SQL block, its execution section immediately terminates. Control is passed to the exception section.

Every exception in PL/SQL has an error number and error message; some exceptions also have names.

Declaring Exceptions

Some exceptions have been predefined by Oracle in the STANDARD package or other built-in packages, such as UTL_FILE. See the following table for many of the common built-in exceptions. You also can declare your own exceptions as follows:

```
DECLARE
    exception_name EXCEPTION;
```

Error	Named exception
ORA-00001	DUP_VAL_ON_INDEX
ORA-00051	TIMEOUT_ON_RESOURCE
ORA-00061	TRANSACTION_BACKED_OUT
ORA-01001	INVALID_CURSOR
ORA-01012	NOT_LOGGED_ON
ORA-01017	LOGIN_DENIED
ORA-01403	NO_DATA_FOUND
ORA-01410	SYS_INVALID_ROWID
ORA-01422	TOO_MANY_ROWS
ORA-01476	ZERO_DIVIDE

Error	Named exception
ORA-01725	USERENV_COMMMITSCN_ERROR
ORA-01722	INVALID_NUMBER
ORA-06500	STORAGE_ERROR
ORA-06501	PROGRAM_ERROR
ORA-06502	VALUE_ERROR
ORA-06504	ROWTYPE_MISMATCH
ORA-06511	CURSOR_ALREADY_OPEN
ORA-06530	ACCESS_INTO_NULL
ORA-06531	COLLECTION_IS_NULL
ORA-06532	SUBSCRIPT_OUTSIDE_LIMIT
ORA-06533	SUBSCRIPT_BEYOND_COUNT
ORA-09592	CASE_NOT_FOUND
ORA-30625	SELF_IS_NULL
ORA-29280	UTL_FILE.INVALID_PATH
ORA-29281	UTL_FILE.INVALID_MODE
ORA-29282	UTL_FILE.INVALID_FILEHANDLE
ORA-29283	UTL_FILE.INVALID_OPERATION
ORA-29284	UTL_FILE.READ_ERROR
ORA-29285	UTL_FILE.WRITE_ERROR
ORA-29286	UTL_FILE.INTERNAL_ERROR
ORA-29287	UTL_FILE.INVALID_MAXLINESIZE
ORA-29288	UTL_FILE.INVALID_FILENAME
ORA-29289	UTL_FILE.ACCESS_DENIED
ORA-29290	UTL_FILE.INVALID_OFFSET
ORA-29291	UTL_FILE.DELETE_FAILED
ORA-29292	UTL_FILE.RENAME_FAILED

An exception can be declared only once in a block, but nested blocks can declare an exception with the same name as an outer block. If this multiple declaration occurs, scope takes precedence over name when handling the exception. The inner block's declaration takes precedence over a global declaration.

When you declare your own exception, you must RAISE it explicitly. All declared exceptions have an error code of 1 and the error message "User-defined exception" unless you use the EXCEPTION_INIT pragma.

You can associate an error number with a declared exception with the PRAGMA EXCEPTION_INIT statement using the following syntax:

```
DECLARE
    exception_name EXCEPTION;
    PRAGMA EXCEPTION_INIT (exception_name, error_number);
```

where *error_number* is a literal value (variable references are not allowed). This number can be an Oracle error, such as -1855, or an error in the user-definable -20000 to -20999 range.

Raising Exceptions

An exception can be raised in three ways:

- By the PL/SQL runtime engine
- By an explicit RAISE statement in your code
- By a call to the built-in function RAISE_APPLICATION_ERROR

The syntax for the RAISE statement is:

```
RAISE exception_name;
```

where *exception_name* is the name of an exception that you have declared, or an exception that is declared in the STANDARD package. If you use the RAISE statement inside an exception handler, you can omit the exception name to re-raise the current exception:

```
RAISE;
```

This syntax is not valid outside the exception section.

The RAISE_APPLICATION_ERROR built-in function has the following header:

```
RAISE_APPLICATION_ERROR (
    num BINARY_INTEGER,
    msg VARCHAR2,
    keeperrorstack BOOLEAN DEFAULT FALSE);
```

where *num* is the error number (an integer between -20999 and -20000), *msg* is the associated error message, and *keeperrorstack* controls whether any previous contents of the error stack are preserved.

Scope

The *scope* of an exception section is that portion of the code that is "covered" by the exception section. An exception handler will handle or attempt to handle only those exceptions that are raised in the executable section of the PL/SQL block. Exceptions raised in the declaration or exception sections are passed to the outer block automatically. Any line or set of PL/SQL code can be placed inside its own block and given its own exception section. This allows you to limit the propagation of an exception.

Propagation

Exceptions raised in a PL/SQL block propagate to an outer block if they are unhandled or re-raised in the exception section. When an exception occurs, PL/SQL looks for an exception handler that checks for the exception (or is the WHEN OTHERS clause) in the current block. If a match is not found, PL/SQL propagates the exception to the enclosing block or calling program. This propagation continues until the exception is handled or propagated out of the outermost block, back to the calling program. In this case, the exception is "unhandled" and (1) stops the calling program, and (2) causes an automatic rollback of any outstanding transactions.

Once an exception is handled, it will not propagate upward. If you want to trap an exception, display a meaningful error message, and have the exception propagate upward as an error, you must re-raise the exception. The RAISE statement can re-raise the current exception or raise a new exception, as shown here:

```
PROCEDURE delete_dept(deptno_in IN NUMBER)
IS
   still_have_employees EXCEPTION;
   PRAGMA EXCEPTION_INIT(still_have_employees, -2292);
BEGIN
   DELETE FROM dept
    WHERE deptno = deptno_in;
EXCEPTION
   WHEN still_have_employees
   THEN
      DBMS_OUTPUT.PUT_LINE
         ('Please delete employees in dept first');
      ROLLBACK;
      RAISE;  --Re-raise the current exception.
END;
```

WHEN OTHERS clause

Use the WHEN OTHERS clause in the exception handler as a catch-all to trap any exceptions that are not handled by specific WHEN clauses in the exception section. If present, this clause must be the last exception handler in the exception section. Specify this clause as follows:

```
EXCEPTION
   WHEN OTHERS
   THEN
      ...
```

SQLCODE and SQLERRM

SQLCODE and SQLERRM are built-in functions that provide the SQL error code and message for the current exception. Use these functions inside the exception section's WHEN OTHERS clause to handle specific errors by number. The EXCEPTION_INIT pragma allows you to handle errors by name. For example, the following code:

```
CREATE TABLE err_test
   (widget_name   VARCHAR2(100)
   ,widget_count  NUMBER
   ,CONSTRAINT no_small_numbers CHECK
      (widget_count > 1000));
BEGIN
   INSERT INTO err_test (widget_name, widget_count)
   VALUES ('Athena',2);
EXCEPTION
   WHEN OTHERS THEN
   IF SQLCODE = -2290
      AND SQLERRM LIKE '%NO_SMALL_NUMBERS%'
   THEN
      DBMS_OUTPUT.PUT_LINE(
       'widget_count is too small');
   ELSE
      DBMS_OUTPUT.PUT_LINE('Exception not handled,'
         ||'SQLcode='||SQLCODE);
      DBMS_OUTPUT.PUT_LINE(SQLERRM);
   END IF;
END;
```

produces this output:

```
widget_count is too small
```

The built-in package DBMS_UTILITY's FORMAT_ERROR_
STACK and FORMAT_CALL_STACK procedures can be
used to capture the full error stack and call stack. See the
book *Oracle Built-in Packages* by Steven Feuerstein, Charles
Dye, and John Beresniewicz (O'Reilly) for more information
on DBMS_UTILITY.

Exceptions and DML

When an exception is raised in a PL/SQL block, it does *not*
roll back your current transaction, even if the block itself
issued an INSERT, UPDATE, or DELETE. You must issue
your own ROLLBACK statement if you want to clean up
your transaction as a result of the exception.

If your exception goes unhandled (propagates out of the
outermost block), however, most host environments, including SQL*Plus, will then force an automatic, unqualified rollback of any outstanding changes in your session.

Records in PL/SQL

A PL/SQL record is a data structure composed of multiple pieces of information called *fields*. To use a record, you must first define it and declare a variable of this type.

There are three types of records: table-based, cursor-based, and programmer-defined.

Declaring Records

You define and declare records either in the declaration section of a PL/SQL block or globally, via a package specification.

You do not have to explicitly define table-based or cursor-based records, as they are implicitly defined with the same structure as a table or a cursor. Variables of these types are declared via the %ROWTYPE attribute. The record's fields correspond to the table's columns or the columns in the SELECT list. For example:

```
DECLARE
    -- Declare table-based record for company table.
    comp_rec   company%ROWTYPE

    CURSOR comp_summary_cur IS
       SELECT c.company_id,SUM(s.gross_sales) gross
         FROM company c ,sales s
        WHERE c.company_id = s.company_id;

    -- Declare a cursor-based record.
    comp_summary_rec  comp_summary_cur%ROWTYPE;
```

Programmer-defined records must be explicitly defined with the TYPE statement in the PL/SQL declaration section or in a package specification. Variables of this type then can be declared as shown here:

```
DECLARE
    TYPE name_rectype IS RECORD(
        prefix        VARCHAR2(15)
        ,first_name   VARCHAR2(30)
        ,middle_name  VARCHAR2(30)
        ,sur_name     VARCHAR2(30)
        ,suffix       VARCHAR2(10) );
```

```
TYPE employee_rectype IS RECORD (
    emp_id      NUMBER(10) NOT NULL
    ,mgr_id     NUMBER(10)
    ,dept_no    dept.deptno%TYPE
    ,title      VARCHAR2(20)
    ,name       name_rectype
    ,hire_date  DATE := SYSDATE
    ,fresh_out  BOOLEAN );

-- Declare a variable of this type.
new_emp_rec employee_rectype;
BEGIN
```

Referencing Fields of Records

Individual fields are referenced via dot notation:

```
record_name.field_name
```

For example:

```
employee.first_name
```

Individual fields within a record can be read from or written to. They can appear on either the left or right side of the assignment operator:

```
BEGIN
    insurance_start_date :=
        new_emp_rec.hire_date + 30;
    new_emp_rec.fresh_out := FALSE;
    ...
```

Assigning Records

An entire record can be assigned to another record of the same type, but one record cannot be compared to another record via Boolean operators. This is a valid assignment:

```
shipto_address_rec := customer_address_rec
```

This is not a valid comparison:

```
IF shipto_address_rec = customer_address_rec
THEN
    ...
END IF;
```

The individual fields of the records need to be compared instead.

Values can be assigned to records or to the fields within a record in four different ways:

- The assignment operator can be used to assign a value to a field:

```
new_emp_rec.hire_date := SYSDATE;
```

- You can SELECT INTO a whole record or the individual fields:

```
SELECT emp_id,dept,title,hire_date,college_recruit
  INTO new_emp_rec
  FROM emp
 WHERE surname = 'LI'
```

- You can FETCH INTO a whole record or the individual fields:

```
FETCH emp_cur INTO new_emp_rec;
FETCH emp_cur
  INTO new_emp_rec.emp_id, new_emp_rec.name;
```

- You can assign all the fields of one record variable to another record variable of the same type:

```
IF rehire THEN
  new_emp_rec := former_emp_rec;
ENDIF;
```

This aggregate assignment technique works only for records declared with the same TYPE statement.

DML and Records

You insert into or update a database table using a %ROWTYPE record without having to specify each field individually in the following ways:

- Insert into a database table, using a %ROWTYPE record and the VALUES keyword:

```
DECLARE
   emp_rec   emp%ROWTYPE;
BEGIN
```

```
            SELECT employees_seq.NEXTVAL
              INTO emp_rec.empno FROM dual;

            INSERT INTO emp VALUES (emp_rec);
         END;
```

- Update a database table using a %ROWTYPE record and the SET ROW keywords:

```
         FOR emp_rec IN emp_cur
         LOOP
            change_record_values(emp_rec);

            UPDATE emp SET ROW = emp_rec
              WHERE empno = emp_rec.empno;
         END LOOP;
```

While these techniques allow you to write more elegant code to interact with a database, you cannot use %ROWTYPE records as bind variables in dynamic SQL.

Nested Records

Nested records are records contained in fields that are records themselves. Nesting records is a powerful way to normalize data structures and hide complexity within PL/SQL programs. For example:

```
     DECLARE
        -- Define a record.
        TYPE phone_rectype IS RECORD (
           area_code   VARCHAR2(3),
           exchange    VARCHAR2(3),
           phn_number  VARCHAR2(4),
           extension   VARCHAR2(4));

        -- Define a record composed of records.
        TYPE contact_rectype IS RECORD (
           day_phone#   phone_rectype,
           eve_phone#   phone_rectype,
           cell_phone#  phone_rectype);

     -- Declare a variable for the nested record.
      auth_rep_info_rec contact_rectype;
     BEGIN
```

Named Program Units

PL/SQL allows you to create a variety of named program units, or containers for code. These include:

Procedure
    A program that executes one or more statements

Function
    A program that returns a value

Package
    A container for procedures, functions, and data structures

Trigger
    A program that executes in response to database changes

Object type
    Oracle's version of an object-oriented class; object types can contain member procedures and functions

Procedures

Procedures are program units that execute one or more statements and can receive or return zero or more values through their parameter lists. The syntax of a procedure is:

```
CREATE [OR REPLACE] PROCEDURE name
   [ (parameter [,parameter]) ]
   [AUTHID { CURRENT_USER | DEFINER } ]
   [DETERMINISTIC]
{ IS | AS }
   declaration_section
BEGIN
   executable_section
[EXCEPTION
   exception_section]
END [name];
```

Inside a PL/SQL executable section, a procedure is called as a standalone executable statement:

```
apply_discount(new_company_id, 0.15);
```

Many execution environments, such as SQL*Plus, also support ANSI SQL's CALL syntax:

```
CALL apply_discount(new_company_id, 0.15);
```

However, SQL*Plus programmers commonly invoke procedures with the SQL*Plus EXECUTE command:

```
EXECUTE apply_discount(new_company_id, 0.15);
```

or the equivalent anonymous block:

```
BEGIN
    apply_discount(new_company_id, 0.15);
END;
```

Functions

Functions are program units that execute zero or more statements and return a value through the RETURN clause. Functions also can receive or return zero or more values through their parameter lists. The syntax of a function is:

```
CREATE [OR REPLACE] FUNCTION name
   [ (parameter [,parameter]) ]
   RETURN return_datatype
   [AUTHID { CURRENT_USER | DEFINER } ]
   [DETERMINISTIC]
   [PARALLEL_ENABLE]
   [PIPELINED]
   [AGGREGATE USING]
{ IS | AS }
   [declaration_section]
BEGIN
   executable_section
[EXCEPTION
   exception_section]
END [name];
```

A function must have at least one RETURN statement in the execution section. The RETURN clause in the function header specifies the datatype of the returned value.

See the "Compiling stored PL/SQL programs" section for information on the keywords OR REPLACE, AUTHID, DETERMINISTIC, PARALLEL_ENABLE, PIPELINED, and

AGGREGATE USING. See the section "Privileges and stored PL/SQL" for additional information on AUTHID.

A function can be called anywhere that an expression of the same type can be used. You can call a function:

- In an assignment statement:
  ```
  sales95 := tot_sales(1995,'C');
  ```
- To set a default value:
  ```
  DECLARE
      sales95 NUMBER DEFAULT tot_sales(1995,'C');
  BEGIN
  ```
- In a Boolean expression:
  ```
  IF tot_sales(1995,'C') > 10000
  THEN
     ...
  ```
- In a SQL statement:
  ```
  SELECT first_name ,surname
      FROM sellers
  WHERE tot_sales(1995,'C') > 1000;
  ```
- As an argument in another program unit's parameter list.

Here, for example, max_discount is a programmer-defined function, and SYSDATE is a built-in function:

```
apply_discount(company_id, max_discount(SYSDATE));
```

Parameters

Procedures, functions, and cursors may have a parameter list. This list contains one or more parameters that allow you to pass information back and forth between the subprogram and the calling program. Each parameter is defined by its name, datatype, mode, and optional default value. The syntax for a parameter is:

```
parameter_name [mode] [NOCOPY] datatype
    [ { := | DEFAULT } value]
```

Datatype

The datatype can be any PL/SQL or programmer-defined datatype, but cannot be constrained by a size (NUMBER is valid, NUMBER(10) is not valid). The actual size of the parameter is determined from the calling program or via a %TYPE constraint.

```
CREATE OR REPLACE PROCEDURE empid_to_name
(in_id          emp.emp_id%TYPE  -- Compiles OK
,out_last_name  VARCHAR2         -- Compiles OK
,out_first_name VARCHAR2(10)     -- Won't compile
) IS
...
```

The lengths of out_last_name and out_first_name are determined by the calling program:

```
DECLARE
    surname    VARCHAR2(10);
    first_name VARCHAR2(10);
BEGIN
    empid_to_name(10, surname, first_name);
END;
```

Mode

The *mode* of a parameter specifies whether the parameter can be read from or written to, as shown in the following table:

Mode	Description	Parameter usage
IN	Read-only	The value of the actual parameter can be referenced inside the program, but the parameter cannot be changed.
OUT or IN OUT	Read/write	The program can both reference (read) and modify (write) the parameter.

If the mode is not explicitly defined, it defaults to IN.

OUT parameters are not the same as IN OUT parameters. When running the called program, the runtime engine ignores (sets to NULL) any argument value you supply for an OUT parameter; it preserves the value provided for an IN OUT. If an exception is raised during execution of a procedure or function, assignments made to OUT or IN OUT parameters get rolled back unless the parameter includes the NOCOPY option.

NOCOPY is a request to the compiler to make the parameter a call by reference instead of a call by value. Normally, PL/SQL passes IN/OUT parameters by value—a copy of the parameter is created for the subprogram. When parameter items get large, as collections and objects do, the copy can eat memory and slow down processing. NOCOPY asks PL/SQL to pass the parameter by reference, using a pointer to the single copy of the parameter.

The main disadvantage of NOCOPY is that when an exception is raised during execution of a program that has modified an OUT or IN OUT parameter, the changes to the actual parameters are not "rolled back" because the parameters were passed by reference instead of being copied. Also, NOCOPY does not always apply; see *Oracle PL/SQL Programming* (O'Reilly) for a list of cases in which the compiler ignores the NOCOPY request.

Default values

IN parameters can be given default values. If an IN parameter has a default value, you do not need to supply an argument for that parameter when you call the program unit. It automatically uses the default value. For example:

```
CREATE OR REPLACE PROCEDURE hire_employee
   (emp_id       IN VARCHAR2
   ,hire_date    IN DATE := SYSDATE
   ,company_id   IN NUMBER := 1
   )
IS
   ...
```

Here are some example calls to the preceding procedure:

```
-- Use two default values.
hire_employee(new_empno);
-- Use one default value.
hire_employee(new_empno,'12-Jan-1999');
-- Use nontrailing default value, named notation.
hire_employee(emp_id=>new_empno, comp_id=>12);
```

Parameter-passing notations

Formal parameters are the names that are declared in the header of a procedure or function. *Actual parameters (arguments)* are the values or expressions placed in the parameter list when a procedure or function is called. In the `empid_to_name` example shown earlier in the "Datatype" section, the formal parameters to the procedure are `in_id`, `out_last_name`, and `out_first_name`. The actual parameters used in the call to this procedure are `10`, `surname`, and `first_name`.

PL/SQL lets you use either of two styles for passing arguments in parameter lists.

Positional notation
> The default. Each value in the list of arguments supplied in the program call is associated with the parameter in the corresponding position.

Named notation
> Explicitly associates the argument value with its parameter by name (not position). When you use named notation, you can supply the arguments in any order, and you can omit IN arguments that have default values.

The call to the `empid_to_name` procedure is shown here with both notations:

```
BEGIN
    -- Implicit positional notation.
    empid_to_name(10, surname, first_name);

    -- Explicit named notation.
    empid_to_name(in_id=>10
        ,out_last_name=>surname
        ,out_first_name=>first_name);
END;
```

You may combine positional and named notation, as long as positional arguments appear to the left of any named notation arguments; for example:

```
    empid_to_name(10, surname, out_first_name => first_name);
```

When calling stored functions from SQL, named notation is not supported.

Local programs

A *local program* is a procedure or function that is defined in the declaration section of a PL/SQL block. The declaration of a local program must appear at the end of the declaration section, after the declarations of any types, records, cursors, variables, and exceptions. A program defined in a declaration section may be referenced only within that block's executable and exception sections. It is not defined outside that block.

The following program defines a local procedure and function:

```
PROCEDURE track_revenue
IS
   l_total NUMBER;

   PROCEDURE calc_total (year_in IN INTEGER) IS
   BEGIN
      calculations here ...
   END;

   FUNCTION below_minimum (comp_id IN INTEGER)
      RETURN BOOLEAN
   IS
   BEGIN
      ...
   END;
BEGIN
   ...main procedure logic here
END;
```

Local programs may be overloaded with the same restrictions as overloaded packaged programs.

Program overloading

PL/SQL allows you to define two or more programs with the same name within any declaration section, including a package specification or body. This is called *overloading*. If two or more programs have the same name, they must be different in some other way so that the compiler can determine which program should be used.

Here is an example of overloaded programs in a built-in package specification:

```
PACKAGE DBMS_OUTPUT
IS
    PROCEDURE PUT_LINE (a VARCHAR2);
    PROCEDURE PUT_LINE (a NUMBER);
    PROCEDURE PUT_LINE (a DATE);
END;
```

Each PUT_LINE procedure is identical, except for the datatype of the parameter. That is enough difference for the compiler.

To overload programs successfully, one or more of the following conditions must be true:

- Parameters must differ by datatype family (number, character, datetime, or Boolean).

- The program type must be different (you can overload a function and a procedure of the same name and identical parameter list).

- The numbers of parameters must be different.

In general, you *cannot* overload programs if:

- Only the datatypes of the functions' RETURN clauses are different.

- Parameter datatypes are within the same family (CHAR and VARCHAR2, NUMBER and INTEGER, etc.).

- Only the modes of the parameters are different.

Oracle Database 10g allows overloading of programs whose parameters differ only in numeric datatypes, as long as they are in different datatype "families." The runtime environment will search first for a matching program with a PLS_INTEGER (or BINARY_INTEGER) parameter, then it will try to match NUMBER, BINARY_FLOAT, and finally BINARY_DOUBLE, in that order. If you want to force the use of the faster IEEE 754 datatypes, you may need to use the TO_BINARY_FLOAT or TO_BINARY_DOUBLE functions on the input argument, or for literals, append with f or d, as discussed in the earlier "Numeric Literals" section.

Forward declarations

Programs must be declared before they can be used. PL/SQL supports *mutual recursion*, in which program A calls program B, whereupon program B calls program A. To implement this mutual recursion, you must use a *forward declaration* of the programs. This technique declares a program in advance of the program definition, thus making it available for other programs to use. The forward declaration is the program header up to the IS/AS keyword:

```
PROCEDURE perform_calc(year_in IN NUMBER)
IS
    /* Forward declaration for total_cost
       function. */
    FUNCTION total_cost (...) RETURN NUMBER;

    /* The net_profit function can now use
       total_cost. */
    FUNCTION net_profit(...) RETURN NUMBER
    IS
    BEGIN
        RETURN total_sales(...) - total_cost(...);
    END;

    /* The total_cost function calls net_profit. */
    FUNCTION total_cost (...) RETURN NUMBER
    IS
    BEGIN
        IF net_profit(...) < 0
        THEN
            RETURN 0;
            ELSE
            RETURN...;
        END IF;
    END;
BEGIN /* procedure perform_calc */
    ...
END perform_calc;
```

Table functions

Table functions take a collection or REF CURSOR (set of rows) as input and return a collection of records (set of rows) as output. The PIPE ROW statement is used to identify the input and output streams. This streamlined nature allows you to pipeline table functions together, eliminating the need to stage tables between transformations. Table functions typically appear in the FROM clause of SQL statements. For example:

```
CREATE OR REPLACE TYPE num_tab_typ AS TABLE OF NUMBER
/

CREATE OR REPLACE FUNCTION piped_func(factor IN NUMBER)
RETURN num_tab_typ
PIPELINED AS
BEGIN
   FOR counter IN 1..1000
   LOOP
     PIPE ROW (counter*factor);
   END LOOP;
END piped_func;
/

SELECT * FROM TABLE(piped_func(2))
WHERE rownum < 5
/
```

Compiling stored PL/SQL programs

The following keywords are available when creating stored programs:

OR REPLACE
> Used to rebuild an existing program unit, preserving privileges granted on it.

AUTHID
> Defines whether the program will execute with the privileges of, and resolve names like, the object owner (DEFINER), or as the user executing the function (CURRENT_USER). Prior to Oracle8i, only the built-in

packages DBMS_SQL and DBMS_UTILITY executed as
CURRENT_USER. The default AUTHID is DEFINER.

DETERMINISTIC

Required for function-based indexes. A function is
DETERMINISTIC if it always returns the same value
when called with the same parameters. Deterministic
functions do not meaningfully reference package variables or the database. The built-in INITCAP is deterministic, but SYSDATE is not.

*PARALLEL_ENABLED [(PARTITION in_parm BY {ANY
HASH | RANGE})]*

Tells the optimizer that a function is safe for parallel execution. The PARTITION BY clause is available only to
functions that have a REF CURSOR IN parameter. This
clause is used with table functions and tells the optimizer how the input can be partitioned.

PIPELINED

Used with table functions. Specifies that the results of
this table function should be returned iteratively via the
PIPE ROW statement. A pipelined function can start to
return data as it is generated instead of all at once after
processing is complete.

AGGREGATE USING

Required for aggregate functions. Tells Oracle that the
function evaluates a group of rows and returns a single
result. For example, the built-in function AVG is an
aggregate function.

Compiler warnings (Oracle Database 10*g*)

Oracle Database 10*g* lets you enable additional compile-time
warnings to help make your programs more robust. These
warnings highlight potential problems that are not severe

enough to raise an exception, but may result in runtime errors or poor performance.

To enable these warnings, you need to set the database initialization parameter PLSQL_WARNINGS. This parameter can be set globally in the *SPFILE* initialization file, in your session via the ALTER SESSION statement, or with the built-in procedure DBMS_WARNING.

The PLSQL_WARNINGS parameter is a comma-delimited list of values, each of which has the syntax:

```
[ENABLE | DISABLE | ERROR] : [ALL | SEVERE | INFORMATIONAL
| PERFORMANCE | warning_number]
```

For example, to enable all warnings in your session, execute:

```
ALTER SESSION SET plsql_warnings = 'enable:all'
```

If you want to enable warning message number 06002 and all warnings in the performance category except warning number 07202, execute:

```
ALTER SESSION SET plsql_warnings = 'enable:06002'
                                  ,'enable:performance'
                                  ,'disable:07202';
```

To see what your current setting is, you can execute:

```
DBMS_OUTPUT.PUT_LINE (
    DBMS_WARNING.get_warning_setting_string( ));
```

Some examples of warnings follow:

```
SQL> ALTER SESSION SET plsql_warnings = 'enable:all';

Session altered.

SQL> CREATE OR REPLACE PACKAGE create_policy IS
2 PROCEDURE process_dec_page ( dec_page IN OUT CLOB );
3 END create_policy;
4 /

SP2-0808: Package created with compilation warnings

SQL> show err
```

```
Errors for PACKAGE CREATE_POLICY:

LINE/COL ERROR
-------- -----------------------------------------------
2/32 PLW-07203: parameter 'DEC_PAGE' may benefit from use
of the NOCOPY compiler hint

SQL> CREATE OR REPLACE PACKAGE BODY create_policy IS
2 PROCEDURE process_dec_page (
3 dec_page IN OUT NOCOPY CLOB ) IS
4 BEGIN
5 default_dec(dec_page);
6 END process_dec_page;
7 END create_policy;
8 /
SP2-0810: Package Body created with compilation warnings

SQL> show err
Errors for PACKAGE BODY CREATE_POLICY:

LINE/COL ERROR
-------- -----------------------------------------------
3/6 PLW-05000: mismatch in NOCOPY qualification between
specification and body

SQL> CREATE OR REPLACE PROCEDURE dead_code IS
2 x NUMBER := 10;
3 BEGIN
4 IF x = 10 THEN
5 x := 20;
6 ELSE
7 x := 100; -- dead code
8 END IF;
9 END dead_code;
10 /

SP2-0804: Procedure created with compilation warnings

SQL> show err
Errors for PROCEDURE DEAD_CODE:

LINE/COL ERROR
-------- -----------------------------------------------
7/7 PLW-06002: Unreachable code
```

The optimizing compiler (Oracle Database 10*g*)

PL/SQL's optimizing compiler, also introduced in Oracle Database 10*g*, can improve runtime performance dramatically while imposing only a relatively slight overhead at compile time. Fortunately, the benefits of optimization apply to both interpreted and natively compiled PL/SQL because optimizations are applied by analyzing patterns in source code.

The optimizing compiler is enabled by default in Oracle Database 10*g*. However, you may want to alter its behavior, by either lowering its aggressiveness or disabling it entirely. For example, if, in the course of normal operations, your system must perform recompilation of many lines of code, or if an application generates many lines of dynamically executed PL/SQL, the overhead of optimization may be unacceptable. Note, however, that Oracle's tests show that the optimizer doubles the runtime performance of computationally intensive PL/SQL.

In some cases, the optimizer may even alter program behavior. One such case might occur in code written for Oracle9*i* that depends on the relative timing of initialization sections in multiple packages. If your testing demonstrates such a problem, yet you want to enjoy the performance benefits of the optimizer, you may want to rewrite the offending code or introduce an initialization routine that ensures the desired order of execution.

To change the optimizer settings for the entire database, set the database parameter PLSQL_OPTIMIZE_LEVEL. Valid settings are:

0   No optimization

1   Moderate optimization, such as eliminating superfluous code or exceptions

2 (default)

> Aggressive optimization beyond level 1, including rearranging source code

You can also modify these settings for the current session; for example:

```
ALTER SESSION SET PLSQL_OPTIMIZE_LEVEL = 0;
```

Oracle retains optimizer settings on a module-by-module basis. When you recompile a particular module with non-default settings, the settings will "stick," allowing you to recompile later using REUSE SETTINGS. For example:

```
ALTER PROCEDURE bigproc COMPILE PLSQL_OPTIMIZE_LEVEL = 0;
```

and then:

```
ALTER PROCEDURE bigproc COMPILE REUSE SETTINGS;
```

To view all of the compiler settings for your modules, including optimizer level, interpreted versus native, and compiler warning levels, query the USER_PLSQL_OBJECT_ SETTINGS view.

Performing native compilation of PL/SQL

Starting with Oracle9*i*, you can speed up many of your PL/SQL programs by compiling the stored programs natively. Oracle will translate your PL/SQL program into C code and compile it into a shared library (DLL on Microsoft Windows platforms). You must have a supported C compiler on your database server machine to use native compilation. You will realize the greatest performance gains with computer-intensive applications. To compile natively in Oracle9*i*, follow these steps:

1. Edit the makefile, *spnc_makefile.mk*, which you should find in the $ORACLE_HOME/plsql subdirectory.

2. Set the initialization parameter PLSQL_COMPILER_FLAGS = 'NATIVE'. Individual developers may alter the value of PLSQL_COMPILER_FLAGS using the ALTER SESSION statement.

3. The following parameters may also need to be set: PLSQL_NATIVE_C_COMPILER, PLSQL_NATIVE_LINKER, PLSQL_NATIVE_LIBRARY_DIR, PLSQL_NATIVE_MAKE_UTILITY, and PLSQL_NATIVE_MAKE_FILE_NAME. The DBA can set these parameters in the Oracle initialization file or using an ALTER SYSTEM statement.

4. If your system has more than approximately 5000 PL/SQL objects, also set PLSQL_NATIVE_DIR_SUBDIR_COUNT and create that many subdirectories (*d0*, *d1*, etc.) under the directory specified by PLSQL_NATIVE_LIBRARY_DIR.

5. Create or replace your stored programs.

6. Verify the native compilation by querying the data dictionary view USER_STORED_SETTINGS and also by locating the shared library or DLL in the database server's filesystem.

In Oracle Database 10*g*, native compilation is much simpler to configure, in part because Oracle now uses database tables rather than files for permanent storage of the generated shared libraries. Oracle also limits support to the C compiler supplied by the platform vendor. To use native compilation in the new release:

1. Inspect the file *$ORACLE_HOME/plsql/spnc_commands* and, if necessary, revise the path to the supported C compiler.

2. Set the parameter PLSQL_NATIVE_LIBRARY_DIR as above and create this directory if it does not exist. This is the location in the filesystem that Oracle will use for an on-demand cache of the shared library files.

3. If your system has more than 15,000 PL/SQL objects, set PLSQL_NATIVE_DIR_SUBDIR_COUNT as above.

4. Either make a global change so that the database parameter PLSQL_CODE_TYPE is set to NATIVE, or issue session-level statements of the form `ALTER SESSION SET PLSQL_CODE_TYPE = 'NATIVE';`.

5. Create or replace your stored programs.

Privileges and stored PL/SQL

Stored SQL supports two models for addressing privileges at runtime. The default is definer rights, which tells Oracle that the privileges of the owner or definer of the program should be used. With the definer rights model, the owner of the program must have the required privileges granted directly to him—he cannot inherit the privileges from a role.

With invoker rights, the user who executes the program does so using his own privileges. Anonymous PL/SQL blocks always execute with invoker rights. To create a program that uses the invoker rights model, include the keywords AUTHID CURRENT_USER in your program's declaration.

Triggers

Triggers are programs that execute in response to changes in table data or certain database events. A predefined set of events can be "hooked" with a trigger, enabling you to integrate your own processing with that of the database. A triggering event *fires* or executes the trigger.

There are three types of triggering events:

- DML events fire when an INSERT, UPDATE, or DELETE statement executes.
- DDL events fire when a CREATE, ALTER, or DROP statement executes.
- Database events fire when one of the predefined database-level events occurs.

Complete lists of these events are included in later sections.

Creating Triggers

The syntax for creating a trigger on a DML event is:

```
CREATE [OR REPLACE] TRIGGER trigger_name
{ BEFORE | AFTER | INSTEAD OF } trigger_event
  ON {table_or_view_reference |
     NESTED TABLE nested_table_column OF view}
     [REFERENCING [OLD AS old] [NEW AS new]
       [PARENT AS parent]]
[FOR EACH ROW ][WHEN trigger_condition]
trigger_body;
```

The syntax for creating a trigger on a DDL or database event is:

```
CREATE [OR REPLACE] TRIGGER trigger_name
{ BEFORE | AFTER } trigger_event
  ON [ DATABASE | schema ]
 [WHEN trigger_condition]
trigger_body;
```

Trigger events are listed in the following table:

Trigger event	Description
INSERT	Fires whenever a row is added to the *table_or_view_reference*.
UPDATE	Fires whenever an UPDATE changes the *table_or_view_reference*. UPDATE triggers can additionally specify an OF clause to restrict firing to updates OF certain columns.
DELETE	Fires whenever a row is deleted from the *table_or_view_reference*. Does not fire on a TRUNCATE of the table.
ALTER	Fires whenever an ALTER statement changes a database object. In this context, objects are things such as tables or packages (found in ALL_OBJECTS). Can apply to a single schema or the entire database.
ANALYZE	Fires whenever the database collects or deletes statistics or validates the structure of a database object.
ASSOCIATE STATISTICS	Fires whenever the database associates a statistic type with a database object.
AUDIT	Fires whenever the database records an audit operation.
COMMENT	Fires whenever a comment on a database object is modified.

Trigger event	Description
CREATE	Fires whenever a database object is created. Does not fire on CREATE CONTROLFILE statements.
DDL	Fires whenever one of the following events occurs: ALTER, ANALYZE, ASSOCIATE STATISTICS, AUDIT, COMMENT, CREATE, DISASSOCIATE, DROP, GRANT, NOAUDIT, RENAME, REVOKE, or TRUNCATE.
DISASSOCIATE STATISTICS	Fires whenever the database disassociates a statistic type from a database object.
DROP	Fires whenever a DROP statement removes an object from the database. In this context, objects are things such as tables or packages (found in ALL_OBJECTS). Can apply to a single schema or the entire database.
GRANT	Fires whenever a system, role, or object privilege is assigned.
NOAUDIT	Fires whenever the database processes a NOAUDIT statement to stop auditing database operations.
RENAME	Fires whenever a RENAME statement changes a database object name.
REVOKE	Fires whenever a system, role, or object privilege is rescinded.
TRUNCATE	Fires whenever a TRUNCATE statement is processed to purge a table or cluster.
SERVERERROR	Fires whenever a server error message is logged. Only AFTER triggers are allowed in this context.
LOGON	Fires whenever a session is created (a user connects to the database). Only AFTER triggers are allowed in this context.
LOGOFF	Fires whenever a session is terminated (a user disconnects from the database). Only BEFORE triggers are allowed in this context.
STARTUP	Fires when the database is opened. Only AFTER triggers are allowed in this context.
SHUTDOWN	Fires when the database is closed. Only BEFORE triggers are allowed in this context.
SUSPEND	Fires whenever a server error causes a transaction to be suspended.

Triggers can fire BEFORE or AFTER the triggering event. AFTER data triggers are slightly more efficient than BEFORE triggers.

The REFERENCING clause is allowed only for the data events INSERT, UPDATE, and DELETE. It lets you give a nondefault name to the old and new pseudorecords. These pseudorecords give the program visibility to the pre- and postchange values in row-level triggers. These records are defined like %ROWTYPE records, except that columns of type LONG or LONG RAW cannot be referenced. They are prefixed with a colon in the trigger body, and referenced with dot notation. Unlike other records, these fields can only be assigned individually—aggregate assignment is not allowed. All old fields are NULL within INSERT triggers, and all new fields are NULL within DELETE triggers.

FOR EACH ROW defines the trigger to be a row-level trigger. Row-level triggers fire once for each row affected. The default is a statement-level trigger, which fires only once for each triggering statement.

The WHEN *trigger_condition* specifies the conditions that must be met for the trigger to fire. Stored functions and object methods are not allowed in the trigger condition.

The trigger body is a standard PL/SQL block. For example:

```
CREATE OR REPLACE TRIGGER add_tstamp
   BEFORE INSERT ON emp
   REFERENCING NEW as new_row
   FOR EACH ROW
   BEGIN
      -- Automatically timestamp the entry.
      SELECT CURRENT_TIMESTAMP
        INTO :new_row.entry_timestamp
        FROM dual;
END add_tstamp;
```

Triggers are enabled on creation, and can be disabled (so that they do not fire) with an ALTER statement, issued with the following syntax:

```
ALTER TRIGGER trigger_name { ENABLE | DISABLE };

ALTER TABLE table_name { ENABLE | DISABLE } ALL TRIGGERS;
```

Trigger Predicates

When using a single trigger for multiple events, use the trigger predicates INSERTING, UPDATING, and DELETING in the trigger condition to identify the triggering event, as shown in this example:

```
CREATE OR REPLACE TRIGGER emp_log_t
   AFTER INSERT OR UPDATE OR DELETE ON emp
   FOR EACH ROW
DECLARE
   dmltype  CHAR(1);
BEGIN
   IF INSERTING THEN
      dmltype := 'I';
      INSERT INTO emp_log (emp_no, who, operation)
         VALUES (:new.empno, USER, dmltype);
   ELSIF UPDATING  THEN
      dmltype := 'U';
      INSERT INTO emp_log (emp_no, who, operation)
         VALUES (:new.empno, USER, dmltype);
   END IF;
END;
```

DML Events

The DML events include INSERT, UPDATE, and DELETE statements on a table or view. Triggers on these events can be statement-level triggers (table only) or row-level triggers and can fire BEFORE or AFTER the triggering event. BEFORE triggers can modify the data in affected rows, but perform an additional logical read. AFTER triggers do not perform this additional logical read, and therefore perform slightly better, but are not able to change the *:new* values. AFTER triggers are thus better suited for data-validation functionality. Triggers cannot be created on SYS-owned objects. The order in which these triggers fire, if present, is as follows:

1. BEFORE statement-level trigger

2. For each row affected by the statement

3. BEFORE row-level trigger

---

4. The triggering statement

5. AFTER row-level trigger

6. AFTER statement-level trigger

DDL Events

The DDL events are ALTER, ANALYZE, ASSOCIATE STA-TISTICS, AUDIT, COMMENT, CREATE, DISASSOCIATE, DROP, GRANT, NOAUDIT, RENAME, REVOKE, and TRUNCATE. These triggers fire whenever the respective DDL statement is executed. DDL triggers can apply to either a single schema or the entire database.

Database Events

The database events are SERVERERROR, LOGON, LOGOFF, STARTUP, SHUTDOWN, and SUSPEND. Only BEFORE triggers are allowed for LOGOFF and SHUT-DOWN events. Only AFTER triggers are allowed for LOGON, STARTUP, and SERVERERROR events. A SHUT-DOWN trigger will fire on a SHUTDOWN NORMAL and a SHUTDOWN IMMEDIATE, but not on a SHUTDOWN ABORT.

Packages

A *package* is a collection of PL/SQL objects that are grouped together. There are several benefits to using packages, including information hiding, object-oriented design, top-down design, object persistence across transactions, and improved performance.

Elements that can be placed in a package include procedures, functions, constants, variables, cursors, exception names, and TYPE statements (for associative arrays [formerly known as index-by tables], records, REF CURSORs, etc.).

Package Structure

A package can have two parts: the specification and the body. The *package specification* is required and lists all the objects that are publicly available (i.e., may be referenced from outside the package) for use in applications. It also provides all the information a developer needs to use objects in the package; essentially, it is the package's API.

The *package body* contains all the code needed to implement procedures, functions, and cursors listed in the specification, as well as any private objects (accessible only to other elements defined in that package), and an optional initialization section.

If a package specification does not contain any procedures or functions, and no private code is needed, that package does not need to have a package body.

The syntax for the package specification is:

```
CREATE [OR REPLACE] PACKAGE package_name
[ AUTHID { CURRENT_USER | DEFINER } ]
{ IS | AS }

   [definitions of public TYPEs
   ,declarations of public variables, types, and objects
   ,declarations of exceptions
   ,pragmas
   ,declarations of cursors, procedures, and functions
   ,headers of procedures and functions]

END [package_name];
```

The syntax for the package body is:

```
CREATE [OR REPLACE] PACKAGE BODY package_name
   { IS | AS }

   [definitions of private TYPEs
   ,declarations of private variables, types, and objects
   ,full definitions of cursors
   ,full definitions of procedures and functions]
```

```
[BEGIN
    executable_statements

[EXCEPTION
    exception_handlers ] ]

END [package_name];
```

The optional OR REPLACE keywords are used to rebuild an existing package, preserving any EXECUTE privileges previously granted to other accounts. The declarations in the specifications cannot be repeated in the body. Both the executable section and the exception section are optional in a package body. If the executable section is present, it is called the *initialization section* and executes only once—the first time any package element is referenced during a session.

You must compile the package specification before the body specification. When you grant EXECUTE authority on a package to another schema or to PUBLIC, you are giving access only to the specification; the body remains hidden.

Here's an example of a package:

```
CREATE OR REPLACE PACKAGE time_pkg IS
    FUNCTION GetTimestamp RETURN DATE;
    PRAGMA RESTRICT_REFERENCES (GetTimestamp, WNDS);

    PROCEDURE ResetTimestamp(new_time DATE
        DEFAULT  SYSDATE);
END time_pkg;

CREATE OR REPLACE PACKAGE BODY time_pkg IS
    StartTimeStamp DATE := SYSDATE;
    -- StartTimeStamp is package data.

    FUNCTION GetTimestamp RETURN DATE IS
    BEGIN
        RETURN StartTimeStamp;
    END GetTimestamp;

    PROCEDURE ResetTimestamp(new_time DATE DEFAULT SYSDATE)
    IS
    BEGIN
```

```
       StartTimeStamp := new_time;
    END ResetTimestamp;

END time_pkg;
```

Referencing Package Elements

The elements declared in the specification are referenced from the calling application via dot notation:

```
package_name.package_element
```

For example, the built-in package DBMS_OUTPUT has a procedure PUT_LINE, so a call to this package would look like this:

```
DBMS_OUTPUT.PUT_LINE('This is parameter data');
```

Package Data

Data structures declared within a package specification or body but outside any procedure or function in the package, are *package data*. The default lifetime of package data is your entire session, spanning transaction boundaries and acting as globals for your programs.

Keep the following guidelines in mind as you work with package data:

- The state of your package variables is not affected by COMMITs and ROLLBACKs.
- A cursor declared in a package has global scope. It remains OPEN until you close it explicitly or until your session ends.
- A good practice is to *hide* your data structures in the package body and provide "get and set" programs to read and write that data. This technique can help protect your data.

SERIALLY_REUSABLE Pragma

If you need package data to exist only during a call to the packaged functions or procedures and not between calls of the current session, you can potentially save runtime memory by using the pragma SERIALLY_REUSABLE. After each call, PL/SQL closes the cursors and releases the memory used in the package. This technique is applicable only to large user communities executing the same routine. Normally, the database server's memory requirements grow linearly with the number of users; with SERIALLY_REUSABLE, this growth can be less than linear because work areas for package states are kept in a pool in Oracle's System Global Area (SGA) and are shared among all users. This pragma must appear in both the specification and the body, as shown here:

```
CREATE OR REPLACE PACKAGE my_pkg IS
   PRAGMA SERIALLY_REUSABLE;
   PROCEDURE foo;
END my_pkg;

CREATE OR REPLACE PACKAGE BODY my_pkg IS
   PRAGMA SERIALLY_REUSABLE;
   PROCEDURE foo IS
   ...
END my_pkg;
```

Package Initialization

The first time a user references a package element, the entire package is loaded into the SGA of the database instance to which the user is connected. That code is then shared by all sessions that have EXECUTE authority on the package.

Any package data is then instantiated into the session's User Global Area (UGA), a private area in either the SGA or the Program Global Area (PGA). If the package body contains an initialization section, that code will be executed. The initialization section is optional and appears at the end of the package body, beginning with a BEGIN statement and ending with the EXCEPTION section (if present) or the END of the package.

The following package initialization section runs a query to transfer the user's minimum balance into a global package variable. Programs can then reference the packaged variable (via the function) to retrieve the balance, rather than execute the query repeatedly:

```
CREATE OR REPLACE PACKAGE usrinfo
IS
    FUNCTION minbal RETURN VARCHAR2;
END usrinfo;
/

CREATE OR REPLACE PACKAGE BODY usrinfo
IS
    g_minbal NUMBER; -- Package data
    FUNCTION minbal RETURN VARCHAR2
    IS
    BEGIN
        RETURN g_minbal;
    END;
BEGIN  -- Initialization section
    SELECT minimum_balance
      INTO g_minbal
      FROM user_configuration
     WHERE username = USER;
EXCEPTION
    WHEN NO_DATA_FOUND
    THEN g_minbal := NULL;
END usrinfo;
```

Calling PL/SQL Functions in SQL

Stored functions can be called from SQL statements in a manner similar to built-in functions such as DECODE, NVL, or RTRIM. This is a powerful technique for incorporating business rules into SQL in a simple and elegant way. Unfortunately, there are several caveats and restrictions.

The most notable caveat is that stored functions executed from SQL are not by default guaranteed to follow the statement-level read consistency model of the database. Unless the SQL statement and any stored functions in that statement are in the same read-consistent transaction (even if they are read-only), each execution of the stored function may look at a different time-consistent set of data. To avoid this potential problem, you need to ensure read consistency programmatically by issuing the SET TRANSACTION READ ONLY or SET TRANSACTION ISOLATION LEVEL SERIALIZABLE statement before executing your SQL statement containing the stored function. A COMMIT or ROLLBACK then needs to follow the SQL statement to end this read-consistent transaction.

Calling a Function

The syntax for calling a stored function from SQL is the same as that used to reference it from PL/SQL:

```
[schema_name.][pkg_name.]func_name[@db_link]
    [parm_list]
```

schema_name is optional and refers to the user/owner of the function or package. *pkg_name* is optional and refers to the package containing the called function. *func_name* is required and is the function name. *db_link* is optional and refers to the database link name to the remote database containing the function. *parm_list* is optional, as are the parameters passed to the function.

The following are example calls to the GetTimestamp function in the time_pkg example seen earlier in the "Package Structure" section:

```
-- Capture system events.
INSERT INTO v_sys_event (timestamp, event, qty_waits)
    SELECT time_pkg.GetTimestamp, event, total_waits
    FROM v$system_event

-- Capture system statistics.
INSERT INTO v_sys_stat (timestamp, stat#, value)
    SELECT time_pkg.GetTimestamp, statistic#, value
    FROM v$sysstat;
```

Requirements and Restrictions

There are several requirements for calling stored functions in SQL:

- All parameters must be IN; no IN OUT or OUT parameters are allowed.

- The datatypes of the function's parameters and RETURN must be compatible with RDBMS datatypes. You cannot have arguments or RETURN types such as BOOLEAN, programmer-defined record, associative array, etc.

- The parameters passed to the function must use positional notation; named notation is not supported.

- The function must be stored in the database, not in a local program, Developer/2000 PL/SQL library, or form.

Calling Packaged Functions in SQL

Prior to Oracle8*i*, it was necessary to assert the purity level of a packaged procedure or function when using it directly or indirectly in a SQL statement. Beginning with Oracle8*i*, the PL/SQL runtime engine determines a program's purity level automatically if no assertion exists. The RESTRICT_REFERENCES pragma is still supported for backward compatibility, but is usually unnecessary.

The RESTRICT_REFERENCES pragma asserts a purity level. The syntax for the RESTRICT_REFERENCES pragma is:

```
PRAGMA RESTRICT_REFERENCES (program_name | DEFAULT,
    purity_level);
```

The keyword DEFAULT applies to all methods of an object type or all programs in a package.

From one to five purity levels, in any order, can be in a comma-delimited list. The *purity level* describes to what extent the program or method is free of *side effects*. Side effects are listed in the following table with the purity levels they address:

Purity level	Description	Restriction
WNDS	Write No Database State	Executes no INSERT, UPDATE, or DELETE statements.
RNDS	Read No Database State	Executes no SELECT statements.
WNPS	Write No Package State	Does not modify any package variables.
RNPS	Read No Package State	Does not read any package variables.
TRUST	—	Does not enforce the restrictions declared, but allows the compiler to trust that they are true.

Column/Function Name Precedence

If your function has the same name as a table column in your SELECT statement, and the function has no parameter, the column takes precedence over the function. To force the RDBMS to resolve the name to your function, prepend the schema name to it:

```
CREATE TABLE emp(new_sal NUMBER ...);
CREATE FUNCTION new_sal RETURN NUMBER IS ...;

SELECT new_sal FROM emp;        -- Resolves to column.
SELECT scott.new_sal FROM emp;  -- Resolves to function.
```

Oracle's Object-Oriented Features

In Oracle, an *object type* combines attributes (data structures) and methods (functions and procedures) into a single programming construct. The object type construct allows programmers to define their own reusable datatypes for use in PL/SQL programs and table and column definitions. An object type must be created in a database before it can be used in a PL/SQL program.

An instance of an object type is an *object* in the same way that a variable is an instance of a scalar type. Objects are either *persistent* (stored in the database) or *transient* (stored only in PL/SQL variables). Objects can be stored in a database as a row in a table (a row object) or as a column in a table. A table of row objects can be created with syntax such as this:

```
CREATE TABLE table_name OF object_type;
```

When stored in such a table, the object (row) has an Object IDentifier (OID) that is unique throughout the database.

Object Types

An object type has two parts: a specification and a body. The specification is required and contains the attributes and method specifications. The syntax for creating the object type specification is:

```
CREATE [OR REPLACE] TYPE obj_type_name
[ AUTHID { CURRENT_USER | DEFINER } ]
{ { IS | AS } OBJECT | UNDER parent_type_name }
(
    attribute_name datatype,...,
    [ [ [NOT] OVERRIDING ] [ [NOT] FINAL ] [ [NOT]
    INSTANTIABLE ] method_spec,...,]
    [PRAGMA RESTRICT_REFERENCES(program_name, purities)]
)
[ [NOT] FINAL ]
[ [NOT] INSTANTIABLE ];
```

where *method_spec* is one of the following:

```
MEMBER { PROCEDURE | FUNCTION } program_spec
```

or:

```
STATIC { PROCEDURE | FUNCTION } program_spec
```

or:

```
{ ORDER | MAP } MEMBER FUNCTION comparison_function_spec
```

or:

```
CONSTRUCTOR FUNCTION constructor_function_spec
```

Attribute specifications must appear before method specifications. Object attributes, like table columns, are defined with a name and a datatype. The name can be any legal identifier, and the datatype can be almost any datatype known to SQL other than LONG, LONG RAW, ROWID, and UROWID. Attributes can be declared using other programmer-defined object types or collection types, but not on the special types ANYTYPE, ANYDATA, or ANYDATASET. Attributes cannot be of datatypes unique to PL/SQL, such as BOOLEAN.

Method headers appear in the object type specification in a comma-delimited list. Unlike in a package specification, commas (not semicolons) terminate the object type program specifications. To support object comparisons and sorting, the type optionally can include one comparison method— either ORDER or MAP. Member methods can be overloaded in object types following the same rules as function and procedure overloading in packages.

Method "specs" that appear earlier in the syntax actually can be call specs for Java classes in the database or for external procedures written in C.

The syntax for creating the object type body is:

```
CREATE [OR REPLACE] TYPE BODY obj_type_name
{ IS | AS }
(
   [ { ORDER | MAP } MEMBER FUNCTION
     comparison_function_body; ]
   [ { MEMBER | STATIC } { FUNCTION | PROCEDURE }
     program_body;]...
)
;
```

Again, the program bodies can be call specs to Java or C programs. The keywords CONSTRUCTOR, UNDER, FINAL, and INSTANTIABLE were all new with Oracle9i.

Type Inheritance

Starting with Oracle9i, you can define subtypes of object types following a single-inheritance model. Oracle does not have a master root-level object; instead, each type is "standalone" unless declared otherwise.

The UNDER keyword specifies that the type exists as a sub-type in a hierarchy. When you are using UNDER, the parent type must be marked NOT FINAL. By default, types are FINAL, meaning that you cannot declare a subtype of that type.

A subtype contains all the attributes and methods of its parent (supertype) and may contain additional attributes and methods. Methods can override corresponding methods from the parent. Changes to the supertype—such as the addition of attributes or methods—are reflected in the subtypes automatically.

By default, object types are INSTANTIABLE—that is, an invoking program may create an object of that type. The phrase NOT INSTANTIABLE tells Oracle that you don't want any objects of the type, in which case Oracle will not create a constructor for it. This variation generally makes sense only with types that will serve as parents of other types.

Methods

There are four kinds of methods: member, static, constructor, and comparison.

Member methods

A *member method* is a procedure or function designated with the keyword MEMBER. Calling programs may invoke such a method only on objects that have been instantiated.

Static methods

A *static method* has no access to a current (SELF) object. Such a method is declared using the keyword STATIC and can be invoked at any time using *type.method* syntax.

Constructor methods

Even if you don't declare any methods, every instantiable object has a default constructor method that allows a calling program to create new objects of that type. This built-in method:

- Has the same name as the object type
- Is a function that returns an object of that type
- Accepts attributes in named or positional notation
- Must be called with a value (or NULL) for every attribute—there is no DEFAULT clause for object attributes
- Cannot be modified

Starting with Oracle9*i*, Oracle programmers can replace this default constructor with their own using the CONSTRUCTOR FUNCTION syntax. This method must have the same name as the object type, but there are no restrictions on its parameter list. The RETURN clause of the constructor's header must be RETURN SELF AS RESULT. Oracle supports the overloading of programmer-defined constructors. All nonstatic methods have the implied parameter SELF, which refers to the current instance of the object. The default mode for the SELF parameter is IN for functions and IN OUT for procedures. A programmer can alter the mode by explicitly including SELF in the formal parameter list. An example of a programmer-defined default constructor follows:

```
CREATE OR REPLACE TYPE book_t AS OBJECT (
    isbn VARCHAR2(13),
    pages INTEGER,

    CONSTRUCTOR FUNCTION book_t (id IN INTEGER DEFAULT
NULL,
        title IN VARCHAR2 DEFAULT NULL,
        isbn IN VARCHAR2 DEFAULT NULL,
        pages IN INTEGER DEFAULT NULL)
        RETURN SELF AS RESULT,

    OVERRIDING MEMBER FUNCTION ck_digit_okay
        RETURN BOOLEAN,

    OVERRIDING MEMBER FUNCTION print
        RETURN VARCHAR2
);
```

Comparison methods

The comparison methods, ORDER and MAP, establish ordinal positions of objects for comparisons such as "<" or "between" and for sorting (ORDER BY, GROUP BY, DISTINCT). Oracle invokes a comparison method automatically whenever it needs to perform such an operation.

MAP and ORDER methods are actually special types of member methods—that is, they execute only in the context of an existing object. An ORDER function accepts two parameters: SELF and another object of the same type. It must return an INTEGER value as explained in the following table:

Return value	Object comparison
Any negative integer (commonly -1)	SELF < second object.
0	SELF = second object.
Any positive integer (commonly 1)	SELF > second object.
NULL	Undefined comparison: attributes needed for the comparison are NULL.

For example, the Senate ranks majority party members higher than nonmajority party members and within the majority (or nonmajority) by years of service. Here is an example ORDER function incorporating these rules:

```
CREATE TYPE senator_t AS OBJECT (
   majority boolean_t,
   yrs_service NUMBER,
   ORDER MEMBER FUNCTION ranking (other IN
      senator_t)
      RETURN INTEGER  );

CREATE OR REPLACE TYPE BODY senator_t AS
   ORDER MEMBER FUNCTION ranking (other IN
      senator_t)
      RETURN INTEGER IS
   BEGIN
      IF SELF.majority.istrue( )
         AND other.majority.istrue( )
```

```
      THEN RETURN SIGN(SELF.yrs_service -
            other.yrs_service);
      ELSIF SELF.majority.istrue( )
         AND other.majority.isfalse( )
      THEN RETURN 1;
      ELSIF SELF.majority.isfalse( )
         AND other.majority.istrue( )
      THEN RETURN -1;
      ELSIF SELF.majority.isfalse( )
         AND other.majority.isfalse( )
      THEN RETURN SIGN(SELF.yrs_service -
            other.yrs_service);
      END IF;
   END ranking;
END;
```

A MAP function accepts no parameters and returns a scalar datatype such as DATE, NUMBER, or VARCHAR2 for which Oracle already knows a collating sequence. The MAP function translates, or *maps*, each object into this scalar datatype space.

If no ORDER or MAP function exists for an object type, SQL, but not PL/SQL, supports only limited equality comparisons of objects. Objects are equal if they are of the same object type and if each attribute is equal.

Use MAP if possible when frequently sorting or comparing a large number of objects, as in a SQL statement; an internal optimization reduces the number of function calls. With ORDER, the function must run once for every comparison.

Methods in Subtypes

Starting with Oracle9*i*, when defining methods in a subtype, you have two options: you can *inherit* a supertype's method, or you can *override* a supertype's method by defining your own subtype method of the same name and parameter list. If you choose to inherit, you do not need to write any code in the subtype.

To override a supertype, you must use the OVERRIDING keyword in the header of the program, as shown here:

```
CREATE TYPE food_t AS OBJECT (
    name VARCHAR2(100),
    food_group  VARCHAR2 (100),
    MEMBER FUNCTION price RETURN NUMBER
    )
    NOT FINAL
    ;
/
CREATE TYPE dessert_t UNDER food_t (
    contains_chocolate CHAR(1),
    OVERRIDING MEMBER FUNCTION price RETURN NUMBER
    )
    ;
/
```

This example also shows that if you want to allow a method to be overridden, you must specify that this method be NOT FINAL. By default, methods are FINAL and cannot be overridden.

You also can define a method to be NOT INSTANTIABLE, which means that you specify only the header of the method, but you do not need to provide an implementation in the OBJECT TYPE body for that method. For example:

```
CREATE TYPE food_t AS OBJECT (
    name VARCHAR2(100),
    food_group  VARCHAR2 (100),
    NOT INSTANTIABLE MEMBER FUNCTION price RETURN NUMBER
    )
    NOT FINAL
    NOT INSTANTIABLE
    ;
/
```

The consequences of a NOT INSTANTIABLE method are as follows:

• The entire object type must be defined as NOT INSTAN-TIABLE, which means that you cannot instantiate an instance from this type. You can use it only as a super-type in an object type hierarchy.

- Any subtype of food_t must provide an implementation of the price function or in turn also be defined as a NOT INSTANTIABLE object type.

Finally, Oracle supports *dynamic method dispatch*, also known as *dynamic polymorphism*, to determine which over-ridden method to invoke at runtime. That is, it will choose the method in the most specific subtype associated with the currently instantiated object.

Manipulating Objects in PL/SQL and SQL

Variables declared as objects begin their life *atomically null*, meaning that the expression:

```
object IS NULL
```

evaluates to TRUE. Attempting to assign values to the attributes of an atomically null object will return an ACCESS_INTO_NULL exception. Instead, you must initialize the object, in one of these ways:

- Use either the default constructor method or a user-defined constructor.
- Assign to it the value of an existing object.
- Use SELECT INTO or FETCH INTO.

Here is an example using each initialization technique:

```
DECLARE
    project_boiler_plate   project_t;
    build_web_site         project_t;

    -- Initialize via constructor.
    new_web_mgr  proj_mgr_t :=
        proj_mgr_t('Ruth', 'Home Office');

    -- Initialize via user-defined constructor
    -- that provides defaults
    new_web_mgr proj_mgr_t := NEW proj_mgr_t();

    CURSOR template_cur IS
      SELECT VALUE(proj)
```

```
      FROM projects
    WHERE project_type = 'TEMPLATE'
      AND  sub_type = 'WEB SITE';
BEGIN
   OPEN template_cur;
   -- Initialize via FETCH INTO.
   FETCH template_cur
      INTO project_boiler_plate;

   -- Initialize via assignment.
   build_web_site := project_boiler_plate;
   ...
```

After an object is initialized, it can be stored in the database, and you can then locate and use that object with the REF, VALUE, and DEREF operators.

Upcasting and Downcasting

Oracle supports implicit *upcasting* (widening) of a subtype and provides the TREAT operator to *downcast* (narrow) a supertype. TREAT also can explicitly upcast a subtype.

The following example returns to the food-dessert hierarchy to demonstrate upcasting and downcasting:

```
CREATE TYPE food_t AS OBJECT (
   name VARCHAR2(100),
   food_group  VARCHAR2 (100)
   )
   NOT FINAL
   ;
/
CREATE TYPE dessert_t UNDER food_t (
   contains_chocolate CHAR(1)
   )
   ;
/

DECLARE
   marzipan dessert_t :=
      NEW dessert_t(marzipan', 'sweets', 'N' );
   ice_cream_sundae dessert_t;
   tasty_treat food_t;
BEGIN
```

```
    /* An implied upcast */
    tasty_treat := marzipan;

    /* An explicit downcast */
    ice_cream_sundae := TREAT(tasty_treat AS dessert_t);
END;
```

The syntax of TREAT is:

```
TREAT (object_instance AS [ REF ] type)
```

where *object_instance* is a value that is of a particular super-type in an object hierarchy, and *type* is the name of the sub-type (or supertype) in the same hierarchy. The TREAT expression won't compile if you attempt to cast a type to another from a different type hierarchy. If you supply an object from the correct type hierarchy, TREAT will return either the casted object or NULL—but not an error.

You also can use dot notation to obtain access to the casted object's attributes and methods:

```
TREAT (object_instance AS type).{ attribute |
    method(args...) } ]
```

SQL also supports TREAT and implied upcasting.

REF operator

REF, short for REFerence, designates a datatype modifier or an operator to retrieve a logical pointer to an object. This pointer encapsulates the OID and can simplify navigation among related database objects. The syntax for a REF operator is:

```
REF(table_alias_name)
```

For example:

```
SELECT REF(p) FROM pets p WHERE ...
```

A PL/SQL variable can hold a reference to a particular object type:

```
DECLARE
    petref REF Pet_t;
BEGIN
    SELECT REF(p) INTO petref FROM pets p WHERE ...
```

Through deletions, REFs can reference a nonexistent object—called a *dangling REF*—resulting in a state that can be detected with the IS DANGLING predicate. For example:

```
UPDATE pets
   SET owner_ref = NULL
 WHERE owner_ref IS DANGLING;
```

Oracle's built-in package UTL_REF provides programmatic access to stored objects via their REF.

VALUE operator

Use the VALUE operator to retrieve a row object as a single object rather than as multiple columns. The syntax for the VALUE operator is:

```
VALUE(table_alias_name)
```

For example:

```
SELECT VALUE(p) FROM pets p WHERE ...
```

DEREF operator

Use the DEREF operator to retrieve the value of an object for which you have a REF. The syntax for DEREF is:

```
DEREF(table_alias_name)
```

For example:

```
DECLARE
   person_ref   REF person_t;
   author       person_t;
BEGIN
   -- Get the ref.
   SELECT REF(p) INTO person_ref
      FROM persons WHERE p.last_name ='Pribyl';

   -- Dereference the pointer back to the value.
   SELECT DEREF(person_ref) INTO author FROM dual;
   ...
```

In addition, Oracle uses an OID internally as a unique key to each object. As with a ROWID, you don't typically use an OID directly.

The following table shows ways of referencing persistent objects:

Scheme	Description	Applications
OID	An opaque, globally unique handle, produced when the object is stored in the database as a table (row) object.	This is the persistent object's handle; it's what REFs point to. Your program never uses it directly.
VALUE	An operator. In SQL, it acts on an object in an object table and returns the object's *contents*. Different from the VALUES keyword found in some INSERT statements.	Used when fetching a table (row) object into a variable, or when you need to refer to an object table as an object instead of a list of columns.
REF	A pointer to an object. May be used within a SQL statement as an operator or in a declaration as a type modifier.	Allows quasi-normalizing of object-relational databases and joining of object tables using dot navigation. In PL/SQL, REFs serve as input/output variables.
DEREF	Reverse pointer lookup for REFs.	Used for retrieving the contents of an object when all you know is its REF.

Changing Object Types

You can add methods, but not attributes, to an object type stored in the database using the ALTER TYPE statement. There are several forms of this statement:

```
ALTER TYPE typename
    { ADD | MODIFY | DROP } ATTRIBUTE attribute_spec
    { INVALIDATE | CASCADE
    { [ NOT ] INCLUDING TABLE DATA |
        CONVERT TO SUBSTITUTABLE }
    [ FORCE ] };

ALTER TYPE typename
    [ NOT ] { INSTANTIABLE | FINAL }
    { INVALIDATE | CASCADE
        { [ NOT ] INCLUDING TABLE DATA |
            CONVERT TO SUBSTITUTABLE }
        [ FORCE ] };
```

```
ALTER TYPE typename
   COMPILE [ DEBUG ] [ SPECIFICATION | BODY ]
             [ REUSE SETTINGS ];
```

Because altering the structure of a type can have quite a few repercussions for database objects, Oracle requires you either to INVALIDATE the dependent objects or to CASCADE the change.

When making a change from FINAL to NOT FINAL and cascading the change, you can cause existing table objects to be either NOT SUBSTITUTABLE (the default) or SUBSTITUTABLE. The following is an example of adding an attribute:

```
ALTER TYPE catalog_item_t
   ADD ATTRIBUTE publication_date VARCHAR2(400)
   CASCADE INCLUDING TABLE DATA;
```

The next example shows adding a method:

```
ALTER TYPE catalog_item_t
   ADD MEMBER PROCEDURE save,
   CASCADE;
```

After adding a method to a spec, you would use CREATE OR REPLACE TYPE BODY to implement it in the body (include all the other methods as well).

There are a variety of restrictions on modifying types; for example, you cannot change a type from INSTANTIABLE to NOT INSTANTIABLE if you have created tables that depend on the type.

The syntax for dropping an object type is:

```
DROP TYPE type_name [FORCE];
```

You can drop only an object type that has not been implemented in a table (or you can drop the tables first). The FORCE option will drop object types even if they have dependencies, but FORCE will irreversibly invalidate any dependent objects such as tables. FORCE does not do a DROP CASCADE.

If you are dropping a type whose parent type has table dependents, this form of the statement:

```
DROP TYPE subtype_name VALIDATE;
```

will "validate" the safety of dropping the subtype before performing it. That is, Oracle will perform the drop only if there are no objects of the subtype in any substitutable columns of the parent type.

Collections

There are three types of collections: associative arrays (formerly known as index-by tables or PL/SQL tables), nested tables, and VARRAYs.

Associative arrays
  Single-dimension, unbounded collections of homogeneous elements available only in PL/SQL, not in the database. Associative arrays are initially sparse; they have nonconsecutive subscripts. There are two types of associative arrays: INDEX BY BINARY_INTEGER, which allows you to associate a value with a BINARY_INTEGER, and INDEX BY VARCHAR2, which allows you to associate a value with a text string.

Nested tables
  Single-dimension, unbounded collections of homogeneous elements available in both PL/SQL and the database as a column of a table. Nested tables initially are dense (they have consecutive subscripts), but they can become sparse through deletions.

VARRAYs
  Variable-size arrays. Single-dimension, bounded collections of homogeneous elements available in both PL/SQL and the database. VARRAYs are never sparse. Unlike nested tables, their element order is preserved when you store and retrieve them from the database.

The following table compares these similar collection types:

	Collection type		
Characteristic	Associative array	Nested table	VARRAY
Dimensionality	Single	Single	Single
Usable in SQL?	No	Yes	Yes
Usable as a column datatype in a table?	No	Yes; data stored "out of line" (in a separate table)	Yes; data typically stored "in line" (in the same table)
Uninitialized state	Empty (cannot be NULL); elements are undefined	Atomically null; illegal to reference elements	Atomically null; illegal to reference elements
Initialization	Automatic, when declared	Via constructor, fetch, assignment	Via constructor, fetch, assignment
In PL/SQL, elements referenced by	BINARY_INTEGER (-2,147,483,647.. 2,147,483,647) or character string (VARCHAR2); maximum length of VARCHAR2 is 30, minimum length is 1	Positive integer between 1 and 2,147,483,647. Elements cannot be referenced unless they have been initialized via the constructor or with the EXTEND function	Positive integer between 1 and 2,147,483,647. Elements cannot be referenced unless they have been initialized via the constructor or with the EXTEND function
Sparse?	Yes	Initially no; after deletions, yes	No
Bounded?	No	Can be extended	Yes
Growing the number of elements in the collection	Assign a value to the element using a new subscript	Elements are added via the constructor or later via the EXTEND method	Elements are added via the constructor or later via the EXTEND method; however, you cannot EXTEND past the upper bound
Shrinking the size of the collection	Automatic	TRIM function	TRIM function

		Collection type	
Can be compared for equality?	No	Yes (in Oracle Database 10g) No (in Oracle9i Release 2 and earlier)	No
Elements retain ordinal position and subscript when stored and retrieved from the database	N/A—can't be stored in database	No	Yes

Declaring a Collection

Collections are implemented as TYPEs. As with any programmer-defined type, you must first define the type, then you can declare instances of that type. The TYPE definition can be stored in the database or declared in the PL/SQL program. Each instance of the TYPE is a collection.

The syntax for declaring an associative array is:

```
TYPE type_name IS TABLE OF element_type [NOT NULL]
   INDEX BY {BINARY_INTEGER | VARCHAR2 (size_limit)};
```

The syntax for a nested table is:

```
[CREATE [OR REPLACE]] TYPE type_name IS TABLE OF
   element_type [NOT NULL];
```

The syntax for a VARRAY is:

```
[CREATE [OR REPLACE]] TYPE type_name IS VARRAY |
   VARYING ARRAY (max_elements) OF element_type
   [NOT NULL];
```

The CREATE keyword defines the statement to be DDL and indicates that this type will exist in the database. The optional OR REPLACE keywords are used to rebuild an existing type, preserving the privileges. *type_name* is any valid identifier that will be used later to declare the collection. *max_elements* is the maximum size of the VARRAY. *element_type* is the type of the collection's elements. All elements are of a single type, which can be most scalar datatypes, an object type, or a REF object type. If the elements are objects, the object type itself cannot have an attribute that is a collection. Explicitly disallowed collection datatypes are BOOLEAN, NCHAR, NCLOB, NVARCHAR2, REF CURSOR, TABLE, and VARRAY.

NOT NULL indicates that a collection of this type cannot have any null elements. However, the collection can be atomically null (uninitialized).

Initializing a Collection

Initializing an associative array is trivial—simply declaring it also initializes it. Initializing a nested table or a VARRAY can be done in any of three ways: explicitly with a constructor, implicitly with a fetch from the database, or implicitly with a direct assignment of another collection variable.

The constructor is a built-in function with the same name as the collection. It constructs the collection from the elements passed to it. The following example shows how you can create a nested table of colors and explicitly initialize it to three elements with a constructor:

```
DECLARE
    TYPE colors_tab_t IS TABLE OF VARCHAR2(30);
    colors_tab colors_tab_t :=
        colors_tab_t('RED','GREEN','BLUE');
BEGIN
```

The next example shows how you can create the nested table of colors and implicitly initialize it with a fetch from the database:

```
-- Create the nested table to exist in the database.
CREATE TYPE colors_tab_t IS TABLE OF VARCHAR2(32);

-- Create table with nested table type as column.
CREATE TABLE color_models
(model_type    VARCHAR2(12)
,colors        color_tab_t)
NESTED TABLE colors STORE AS
    color_model_colors_tab;
```

```
-- Add some data to the table.
INSERT INTO color_models
   VALUES('RGB',color_tab_t('RED','GREEN','BLUE'));
INSERT INTO color_models
   VALUES('CYMK',color_tab_t('CYAN','YELLOW',
      'MAGENTA' 'BLACK'));

-- Initialize a collection of colors from the table.
DECLARE
   basic_colors colors_tab_t;
BEGIN
   SELECT colors INTO basic_colors
     FROM color_models
    WHERE model_type = 'RGB';
...
END;
```

The third example shows how you can implicitly initialize the table via an assignment from an existing collection:

```
DECLARE
   basic_colors Color_tab_t :=
      Color_tab_t ('RED','GREEN','BLUE');

   my_colors Color_tab_t;
BEGIN
   my_colors := basic_colors;
   my_colors(2) := 'MUSTARD';
```

Adding and Removing Elements

Elements in an associative array can be added simply by referencing new subscripts. To add elements to nested tables or VARRAYs, you must first enlarge the collection with the EXTEND function, and then you can assign a value to a new element using one of the methods described in the previous section.

Use the DELETE function to remove an element in a nested table regardless of its position. The TRIM function also can be used to remove elements, but only from the end of a collection. To avoid unexpected results, do not use both DELETE and TRIM on the same collection.

Nested Table Functions

Several functions can be used to manipulate collections.

Note that COLLECT is valid only in a SQL statement; it cannot be used, for example, in a PL/SQL assignment.

NOTE

Most of these functions are new to Oracle Database 10g; only CAST and MULTISET are available in earlier releases.

The following table describes these collection (multiset) functions:

Function	Return value	Description
=	BOOLEAN	Compares two nested tables and returns TRUE if they have the same named type and cardinality and if the elements are equal.
<>	BOOLEAN	Compares two nested tables and returns FALSE if they differ in named type, cardinality, or equality of elements.
[NOT] IN ( )	BOOLEAN	Returns TRUE [FALSE] if the nested table to the left of IN exists in the list of nested tables specified in the parentheses.
CARDINALITY(x)	NUMBER	Returns the number of elements in VARRAY or nested table x. Returns NULL if the collection is atomically NULL (not initialized).
CAST(k AS t)	TYPE t	Changes the datatype of k to type t; used in conjunction with COLLECT or MULTISET.
COLLECT	NESTED TABLE	Used in conjunction with CAST to map a column to a collection.
MULTISET	NESTED TABLE	Used in conjunction with CAST to map a subquery to a collection.

Function	Return value	Description
x MULTISET EXCEPT [DISTINCT] y	NESTED TABLE	Performs a MINUS set operation on nested tables x and y, returning a nested table whose elements are in x, but not in y. x, y and the returned nested table must all be of the same type. The DISTINCT keyword forces the elimination of duplicates from the returned nested table.
x MULTISET INTERSECT [DISTINCT] y	NESTED TABLE	Performs an INTERSECT set operation on nested tables x and y, returning a nested table whose elements are in both x and y. x, y, and the returned nested table must all be of the same type. The DISTINCT keyword forces the elimination of duplicates from the returned nested table.
x MULTISET UNION [DISTINCT] y	NESTED TABLE	Performs a UNION set operation on nested tables x and y, returning a nested table whose elements include all those in x as well as those in y. x, y, and the returned nested table must all be of the same type. The DISTINCT keyword forces the elimination of duplicates from the returned nested table.
SET(x)	NESTED TABLE	Returns nested table x without duplicate elements.
x IS [NOT]A SET	BOOLEAN	Returns TRUE [FALSE] if the nested table x is composed of unique elements.
x IS [NOT] EMPTY	BOOLEAN	Returns TRUE [FALSE] if the nested table x is empty.
e [NOT] MEMBER [OF] x	BOOLEAN	Returns TRUE [FALSE] if an expression e is a member of the nested table x.
y [NOT] SUBMULTISET [OF] x	BOOLEAN	Returns TRUE [FALSE] if nested table y contains only elements that are also in nested table x.

The CAST function works together with the COLLECT and MULTISET functions. MULTISET was available prior to Oracle Database 10g and operates on a subquery. COLLECT is new in Oracle Database 10g and operates on a column in a SQL statement:

```
CREATE TYPE email_list_t AS TABLE OF VARCHAR2(64);

-- COLLECT operates on a column
SELECT CAST(COLLECT(cust_email)AS email_list_t)
FROM oe.customers;

-- which is equivalent to
SELECT CAST(MULTISET(SELECT cust_email
                     FROM oe.customers)
            AS email_list_t)
FROM dual;
```

The following provides examples of the other nested table functions, operators, and expressions:

```
DECLARE
  TYPE nested_type IS TABLE OF NUMBER;
  nt1 nested_type := nested_type(1,2,3);
  nt2 nested_type := nested_type(3,2,1);
  nt3 nested_type := nested_type(2,3,1,3);
  nt4 nested_type := nested_type(1,2,4);
  answer nested_type;
BEGIN
  answer := nt1 MULTISET UNION nt4; -- (1,2,3,1,2,4)
  answer := nt1 MULTISET UNION nt3; -- (1,2,3,2,3,1,3)
  answer := nt1 MULTISET UNION DISTINCT nt3; -- (1,2,3)
  answer := nt2 MULTISET INTERSECT nt3; -- (3,2,1)
  answer := nt2 MULTISET INTERSECT DISTINCT nt3;
    -- (3,2,1)
  answer := nt3 MULTISET EXCEPT nt2; -- (3)
  answer := nt3 MULTISET EXCEPT DISTINCT nt2; -- ( )
  answer := SET(nt3); -- (2,3,1)
  IF (nt1 IS A SET) AND (nt3 IS NOT A SET) THEN
     dbms_output.put_line('nt1 has unique elements');
     dbms_output.put_line('but nt3 does not');
  END IF;
  IF (nt3 MULTISET EXCEPT DISTINCT nt2) IS EMPTY THEN
     dbms_output.put_line('empty set');
  END IF;
```

```
IF 3 MEMBER OF (nt3 MULTISET EXCEPT nt2) THEN
   dbms_output.put_line('3 is in the answer set');
END IF;
IF nt1 SUBMULTISET nt3 THEN
   dbms_output.put_line('nt1 is a subset of nt3');
END IF;
IF SET(nt3) IN (nt1,nt2,nt3)  THEN
   dbms_output.put_line(
      'expression is IN the list of nested tables');
END IF;
END;
```

Collection Methods

Several built-in functions (methods) are defined for all collections. These methods are called with dot notation:

```
collection_name.method_name[(parameters)]
```

The methods are listed in the following table:

Collection method	Description
COUNT	A function. Returns the current number of elements in the collection. If a collection is atomically NULL, this method raises an exception. Consider the CARDINALITY( ) function instead.
DELETE [(i[,j])]	A procedure. Removes element i or elements i through j from a nested table or associative array. When called with no parameters, removes all elements in the collection. Reduces the COUNT if the element is not already DELETEd. Does not apply to VARRAYs.
EXISTS (i)	A function. Returns TRUE or FALSE to indicate whether element i exists. If the collection is an uninitialized nested table or VARRAY, returns FALSE.
EXTEND [(n [,i])]	A procedure. Appends n elements to a collection, initializing them to the value of element i. n is optional and defaults to 1.
FIRST	A function. Returns the lowest index in use. Returns NULL when applied to empty initialized collections.
LAST	A function. Returns the greatest index in use. Returns NULL when applied to empty initialized collections.
LIMIT	A function. Returns the maximum number of allowed elements in a VARRAY. Returns NULL for associative arrays and nested tables.

Collection method	Description
PRIOR (*i*)	A function. Returns the index immediately before element *i*. Returns NULL if *i* is less than or equal to FIRST.
NEXT (*i*)	A function. Returns the index immediately after element *i*. Returns NULL if *i* is greater than or equal to COUNT.
TRIM [(*n*)]	A procedure. Removes *n* elements at the end of the collection with the largest index. *n* is optional and defaults to 1. If *n* is NULL, TRIM does nothing. Associative arrays cannot be TRIMmed.

The EXISTS function returns a BOOLEAN, and all other functions and procedures return BINARY_INTEGER except for collections indexed by VARCHAR2, which can return character strings. All parameters are of the BINARY_INTEGER type. Only EXISTS can be used on uninitialized nested tables or VARRAYs. Other methods applied to these atomically null collections will raise the COLLECTION_IS_NULL exception.

DELETE and TRIM both remove elements from a nested table, but TRIM also removes the placeholder, while DELETE does not. This behavior may be confusing because TRIM can remove previously DELETEd elements.

Here is an example of some collection methods in use with an associative array:

```
DECLARE
    TYPE population_type IS
        TABLE OF NUMBER INDEX BY VARCHAR2(64);
    continent_population population_type;
    howmany NUMBER;
    continent_name VARCHAR2(64);
BEGIN
    continent_population('Australia') := 30000000;
    -- Create new entry
    continent_population('Antarctica') := 1000;
    -- Replace old value
    continent_population('Antarctica') := 1001;
    continent_name := continent_population.FIRST;
    DBMS_OUTPUT.PUT_LINE (continent_name);
```

```
      DBMS_OUTPUT.PUT_LINE (
          continent_population(continent_name));
      continent_name := continent_population.LAST;
      DBMS_OUTPUT.PUT_LINE (continent_name);
      DBMS_OUTPUT.PUT_LINE
          (continent_population(continent_name));
   END;
   /
```

This example produces the following output:

```
Antarctica
1001
Australia
30000000
```

Here is an example of some collection methods in use with a
nested table:

```
DECLARE
   TYPE colors_tab_t IS TABLE OF VARCHAR2(30);
   my_list colors_tab_t :=
      colors_tab_t('RED','GREEN','BLUE');
   element BINARY_INTEGER;
BEGIN
   DBMS_OUTPUT.PUT_LINE('my_list has '
      ||my_list.COUNT||' elements');
   my_list.DELETE(2); -- delete element two
   DBMS_OUTPUT.PUT_LINE('my_list has '
      ||my_list.COUNT||' elements');

   FOR element IN my_list.FIRST..my_list.LAST
   LOOP
      IF my_list.EXISTS(element)
      THEN
         DBMS_OUTPUT.PUT_LINE(my_list(element)
            || ' Prior= '||my_list.PRIOR(element)
            || ' Next= ' ||my_list.NEXT(element));
      ELSE
         DBMS_OUTPUT.PUT_LINE('Element '|| element
            ||' deleted. Prior= '||my_
               list.PRIOR(element)
            || ' Next= '||my_list.NEXT(element));
      END IF;
   END LOOP;
END;
```

The previous example produces the following output:

```
my_list has 3 elements
my_list has 2 elements
RED Prior= Next= 3
Element 2 deleted. Prior= 1 Next= 3
BLUE Prior= 1 Next=
```

Collections and Privileges

As with other TYPEs in the database, you need the EXE-CUTE privilege on that TYPE to use a collection type created by another schema (user account) in the database.

Note that Oracle9i Release 2 made it possible to use synonyms for user-defined TYPE names.

Nested Collections

Nested collections, introduced in Oracle9i, are collections contained in members that are collections themselves. Nesting collections is a powerful way to implement object-oriented programming constructs within PL/SQL programs. For example:

```
CREATE TYPE books IS TABLE OF VARCHAR2(64);
CREATE TYPE our_books IS TABLE OF books;
```

Bulk Binds

You can use collections to improve the performance of SQL operations executed iteratively by using *bulk binds*. Bulk binds reduce the number of context switches between the PL/SQL engine and the SQL engine. Two PL/SQL language constructs implement bulk binds: FORALL and BULK COL-LECT INTO.

The syntax for the FORALL statement is:

```
FORALL bulk_index IN [lower_bound..upper_bound
  | INDICES OF collection_variable[BETWEEN lower_bound AND
  upper_bound]
```

```
| VALUES OF collection_variable ]
[SAVE EXCEPTIONS]
sql_statement;
```

bulk_index can be used only in the *sql_statement* and only as a collection index (subscript). When PL/SQL processes this statement, the whole collection, instead of each individual collection element, is sent to the database server for processing. To delete all the accounts in the collection named inactives from the table ledger, do this:

```
FORALL i IN inactives.FIRST..inactives.LAST
    DELETE FROM ledger WHERE acct_no = inactives(i);
```

With Oracle Database 10g, if nonconsecutive index values result from deletions, you will need to use the INDICES OF syntax to skip over the deleted elements:

```
FORALL i IN INDICES OF inactives
    DELETE FROM ledger WHERE acct_no = inactives(i);
```

With Oracle Database 10g, if you are interested in the values of a sparse collection of integers instead of the indices, you will need to use the VALUES OF syntax:

```
FORALL i IN VALUES OF inactives_list
    -- inactives_list is a collection of index values from
    -- the inactives table which are earmarked for deletion
    DELETE FROM ledger WHERE acct_no = inactives(i);
```

These new INDICES OF and VALUES OF keywords allow you to specify a subset of rows in a driving collection that will be used in the FORALL statement. To match the row numbers in the data collection with the row numbers in the driving collection, use the INDICES OF clause. To match the row numbers in the data collection with the values found in the defined rows of the driving collection, use the VALUES OF clause.

The default is for Oracle to stop after the first exception encountered. Use the keywords SAVE EXCEPTIONS to tell Oracle that processing should continue after encountering exceptions. The cursor attribute %BULK_EXCEPTIONS stores a collection of records containing the errors. These records have two fields, EXCEPTION_INDEX and EXCEPTION_CODE, which contain the FORALL iteration during which the exception was raised, as well as the SQLCODE for the exception. If no exceptions are raised, the SQL%BULK_EXCEPTIONS.COUNT method returns 0. For example:

```
DECLARE
  TYPE NameList IS TABLE OF VARCHAR2(32);
  name_tab NameList := NameList('Pribyl'
          ,'Dawes','Feuerstein','Gennick'
          ,'Pribyl','Beresniewicz','Dawes','Dye');
  error_count NUMBER;
  bulk_errors EXCEPTION;
  PRAGMA exception_init(bulk_errors, -24381);
BEGIN
  FORALL indx IN name_tab.FIRST..name_tab.LAST SAVE
EXCEPTIONS
    INSERT INTO authors (name) VALUES (name_tab(indx));
    -- authors has pk index on name
  EXCEPTION
    WHEN others THEN
      error_count := SQL%BULK_EXCEPTIONS.COUNT;
      DBMS_OUTPUT.PUT_LINE('Number of errors is ' ||
          error_count);
      FOR indx IN 1..error_count LOOP
        DBMS_OUTPUT.PUT_LINE('Error ' || indx || '
            occurred during '||'iteration ' ||
             SQL%BULK_EXCEPTIONS(indx).ERROR_INDEX);
        DBMS_OUTPUT.PUT_LINE('Error is ' ||
           SQLERRM(-SQL%BULK_EXCEPTIONS(indx).ERROR_CODE));
      END LOOP;
END;
/

Number of errors is 2
Error 1 occurred during iteration 5
Error is ORA-00001: unique constraint (.) violated
Error 2 occurred during iteration 7
Error is ORA-00001: unique constraint (.) violated
```

The syntax for the BULK COLLECT INTO clause is:

```
BULK COLLECT INTO collection_name_list;
```

where *collection_name_list* is a comma-delimited list of collections, one for each column in the SELECT. Collections of records cannot be a target of a BULK COLLECT INTO clause. However, Oracle does support retrieving a set of typed objects and "bulk collecting" them into a collection of objects.

The BULK COLLECT INTO clause can be used in SELECT INTO, FETCH INTO, or RETURNING INTO statements. For example:

```
DECLARE
    TYPE vendor_name_tab IS TABLE OF
        vendors.name%TYPE;
    TYPE vendor_term_tab IS TABLE OF
        vendors.terms%TYPE;
    v_names vendor_name_tab;
    v_terms vendor_term_tab;
BEGIN
    SELECT name, terms
      BULK COLLECT INTO v_names, v_terms
      FROM vendors
     WHERE terms < 30;
    ...
END;
```

The next function deletes products in an input list of categories, and the SQL RETURNING clause returns a list of deleted products:

```
FUNCTION cascade_category_delete (categorylist clist_t)
RETURN prodlist_t
IS
    prodlist prodlist_t;
BEGIN
    FORALL aprod IN categorylist.FIRST..categorylist.LAST
        DELETE FROM product WHERE product_id IN
            categorylist(aprod)
        RETURNING product_id BULK COLLECT INTO prodlist;
    RETURN prodlist;
END;
```

You can use the SQL%BULK_ROWCOUNT cursor attribute for bulk bind operations. It is like an associative array containing the number of rows affected by the

executions of the bulk bound statements. The *n*th element of
SQL%BULK_ROWCOUNT contains the number of rows
affected by the *n*th execution of the SQL statement. For
example:

```
FORALL i IN inactives.FIRST..inactives.LAST
   DELETE FROM ledger WHERE acct_no = inactives(i);
FOR counter IN inactives.FIRST..inactives.LAST
LOOP
   IF SQL%BULK_ROWCOUNT(counter) = 0
   THEN
      DBMS_OUTPUT.PUT_LINE('No rows deleted for '||
         counter);
   END IF;
END LOOP;
```

You cannot pass SQL%BULK_ROWCOUNT as a parameter to another program, or use an aggregate assignment to
another collection. %ROWCOUNT contains a summation
of all %BULK_ROWCOUNT elements. %FOUND and
%NOTFOUND reflect only the last execution of the SQL
statement.

External Procedures

External procedures provide a mechanism for calling out to a
nondatabase program, such as a DLL under NT or a shared
library under Unix. Every session calling an external procedure will have its own *extproc* process started by the listener.
This *extproc* process is started with the first call to the external procedure and terminates when the session exits. The
shared library needs to have a corresponding library created
for it in the database.

Creating an External Procedure

The following are the steps you need to follow to create an
external procedure.

Set up the listener

External procedures require a listener. If you are running an Oracle Net database listener, it can be used as the *extproc* listener as well, although you may increase security by separating it from the external procedure listener and launching it from a privilege-limited account. Here is one way to structure the *listener.ora* file:

```
LISTENER =
  (ADDRESS = (PROTOCOL=TCP)(HOST=hostname)(PORT=1521))

EXTPROC_LISTENER =
  (ADDRESS = (PROTOCOL = IPC)(KEY = extprocKey))

SID_LIST_LISTENER =
  (SID_DESC =
    (GLOBAL_DBNAME = global_name)
    (ORACLE_HOME = oracle_home_directory)
    (SID_NAME = SID)
  )

SID_LIST_EXTPROC_LISTENER =
  (SID_DESC =
    (SID_NAME = extprocSID)
    (ORACLE_HOME = oracle_home_directory)
    (ENVS = "EXTPROC_DLLS=
      qualifier:shared_object_file_list")
    (PROGRAM = extproc)
  )
```

where:

extprocKey

Short identifier used by Oracle Net to distinguish this listener from other potential IPC listeners. Its actual name is arbitrary because your programs will never see it. Oracle uses EXTPROC0 as the default name for the first Oracle Net installation on a given machine. This identifier must be the same in the address list of the *listener.ora* and *tnsnames.ora* files.

extprocSID

> Arbitrary unique identifier for the external procedure listener. In the default installation, Oracle uses the value PLSExtProc.

ENVS

> Means of passing environment variables to the external procedure listener. The previous example shows only one name/value pair, but any number of pairs are permitted. Use *name=value* syntax, separating each name/value pair with a comma, as in:
>
> ```
> (ENVS="LD_LIBRARY_PATH=
>     /lib:/oracle/product/9.2/lib,EXTPROC_DLLS=ANY")
> ```

EXTPROC_DLLS

> Environment variable designating nondefault locations of shared libraries/DLLs. Without this setting, the default security settings of Oracle9*i* Release 2 require the library/DLL to be in the *bin* subdirectory on Windows platforms, and in Oracle's *lib* subdirectory on Unix. The *qualifier* is actually optional; if it is not present, the additional files given in a colon-delimited *shared_object_file_list* are allowed. If *qualifier* is present, it must be one of the keywords ALL (no location checking) or ONLY (disallows the default locations).

Here is an example ENVS entry supporting two shared libraries found in nondefault locations:

```
(ENVS="EXTPROC_DLLS=ONLY:/u01/app/oracle/admin/local/lib/
    extprocsh.so:/u01/app/oracle/admin/local/lib/
    RawdataToPrinter.so")
```

Installations unconcerned with security may wish to permit any location using an entry such as the following:

```
(ENVS="EXTPROC_DLLS=ALL")
```

See the *Oracle Database 10g Application Developers Guide—Fundamentals* or the *Oracle Database 10g Net Services Administrators Guide* for more details on configuring external procedures and your listener.

Identify or create the shared library or DLL

This step has nothing to do with PL/SQL and may or may not have anything to do with the database. You must write your own C routines and link them into a shared library/DLL or use an existing library's functions or procedures. In the simple example in the next section, we will use the existing random-number-generating calls available from the operating system.

Create the library in the database

Create a library in the database for the shared library or DLL using the CREATE LIBRARY statement:

```
CREATE [OR REPLACE] LIBRARY library_name
{ IS | AS }
   'absolute_path_and_file'
   [ AGENT 'agent_db_link'];
```

The optional AGENT clause represents a database link associated with the service name of an external procedure listener. In this way, the library can invoke a separate runtime instantiation of the *extproc* process. This process can run on a different database server, although that server still must reside on the same machine as the calling program.

To remove libraries from the database, use the DROP LIBRARY statement:

```
DROP LIBRARY library_name;
```

To call out to the C runtime library's *rand* function, you don't have to code any C routines at all because the call is already linked into a shared library and because its arguments are directly type-mappable to PL/SQL. If the *rand* function is in the standard */lib/libc.so* shared library, as on Solaris, you would issue the following CREATE LIBRARY statement:

```
CREATE OR REPLACE LIBRARY libc_l AS
   '/lib/libc.so';  -- References C runtime library.
```

This is the typical corresponding statement for Microsoft Windows:

```
CREATE OR REPLACE LIBRARY libc_l AS
    'C:\WINDOWS\SYSTEM32\CRTDLL.DLL';
```

Create the PL/SQL wrapper
for the external procedure

The syntax for the wrapper procedure is:

```
CREATE [OR REPLACE] PROCEDURE proc_name
    [parm_list]
{ AS | IS } LANGUAGE C
    [NAME external_name]    LIBRARY library_name
    [ AGENT IN (formal_parameter_name) ]
    [WITH CONTEXT]
    [PARAMETERS (external_parameter_list)];
```

where:

proc_name
    The name of the wrapper procedure.

library_name
    The name of the library created with the CREATE LIBRARY statement.

agent_name
    A way of designating a different agent process, similar to the AGENT clause on the library, but deferring the selection of the agent until runtime. You will pass in the value of the agent as a formal PL/SQL parameter to the call spec; it will supersede the name of the agent given in the library, if any.

external_name
    The name of the external routine as it appears in the library. It defaults to the wrapper package name. PL/SQL package names usually are saved in uppercase, so the *external_name* may need to be enclosed in double quotes to preserve case.

WITH CONTEXT
> Used to pass a context pointer to the external routine, so it can make Oracle Call Interface (OCI) calls back to the database.

PARAMETERS
> Identifies the *external_parameter_list*, which is a comma-delimited list containing the position and datatype of parameters that get passed to the external routine. For more details on the *external_parameter_list*, see the next section, "Parameters."

The wrapper PL/SQL function or procedure is often in a package. Using the preceding random-number-generator example, we could create the wrapper package as follows:

```
CREATE OR REPLACE PACKAGE random_utl
AS
    FUNCTION rand RETURN PLS_INTEGER;
    PRAGMA RESTRICT_REFERENCES(rand,WNDS,RNDS,WNPS,RNPS);

    PROCEDURE srand (seed IN PLS_INTEGER);
    PRAGMA RESTRICT_REFERENCES(srand,WNDS,RNDS,WNPS,RNPS);
END random_utl;

CREATE PACKAGE BODY random_utl
AS
    FUNCTION rand RETURN PLS_INTEGER
    IS
        LANGUAGE C      -- Language of routine.
        NAME "rand"     -- Function name in the C program.
        LIBRARY libc_l; -- The library created above.

    PROCEDURE srand (seed IN PLS_INTEGER)
    IS
        LANGUAGE C
        NAME "srand"
        LIBRARY libc_l
        PARAMETERS (seed ub4); --Map to unsigned INT
END random_utl;
```

To use this external random number function, we simply call the package procedure srand to seed the generator, then the package function rand to get random numbers.

```
DECLARE
   random_nbr   PLS_INTEGER;
   seed         PLS_INTEGER;
BEGIN
   SELECT TO_CHAR(SYSDATE,'SSSSS') INTO seed
      FROM dual;

   random_utl.srand(seed);  -- Seed the generator.

   random_nbr := random_utl.rand; -- Get the number.
   DBMS_OUTPUT.PUT_LINE('number='||random_nbr);

   random_nbr := random_utl.rand; -- Get the number.
   DBMS_OUTPUT.PUT_LINE('number='||random_nbr);
END;
```

You can generate random numbers without the complexity or overhead of an external call by using the built-in package DBMS_RANDOM. To learn more about DBMS_RANDOM and other built-ins, check out *Oracle Built-in Packages*.

Parameters

When it comes to passing PL/SQL variables to C variables, we encounter many inconsistencies. For example, PL/SQL supports nullity, while C does not; PL/SQL can have variables in different character sets, while C cannot; and the datatypes in PL/SQL do not directly map to C datatypes.

The PARAMETERS clause specifies the external parameter list, a comma-delimited list containing parameters. The syntax for these parameters (other than CONTEXT) is:

```
{ pname | RETURN | SELF } [ property ] [ BY REFERENCE ]
   [ external_datatype ]
```

If your call spec includes WITH CONTEXT, the corresponding element in the parameter list is simply:

```
CONTEXT
```

The keyword CONTEXT indicates the position in the parameter list at which the context pointer will be passed. By convention, CONTEXT appears as the first parameter in the external parameter list.

The keyword RETURN indicates that the descriptions are for the return value from the external routine. By default, RETURN is passed by value. You can use the keywords BY REFERENCE to pass by reference (use pointers).

parameter_name is a PL/SQL formal parameter name. By default, IN formal parameters are passed by value. You can use the keywords BY REFERENCE to pass by reference (as a pointer). IN OUT and OUT formal parameters always are passed by reference.

property breaks out further to the general syntax:

```
INDICATOR | INDICATOR STRUCT | LENGTH | MAXLEN | TDO |
CHARSETID | CHARSETFORM
```

INDICATOR indicates whether the corresponding parameter is NULL. In the C program, if the indicator equals the constant OCI_IND_NULL, the parameter is NULL. If the indicator equals the constant OCI_IND_NOTNULL, the indicator is not NULL. For IN parameters, INDICATOR is passed by value (by default). For IN OUT, OUT, and RETURN parameters, INDICATOR is passed by reference.

You can pass a user-defined type to an external procedure. To do so, you will typically pass three parameters: the actual object value; a Type Descriptor Object (TDO) parameter as defined in C by the Oracle Type Translator; and an INDICATOR STRUCT parameter, to designate whether the object is NULL.

LENGTH and MAXLEN can be used to pass the current and maximum length of strings or RAWs. For IN parameters, LENGTH is passed by value (by default). For IN OUT, OUT, and RETURN parameters, LENGTH is passed by reference. MAXLEN is not valid for IN parameters. For IN OUT, OUT, and RETURN parameters, MAXLEN is passed by reference and is read-only.

CHARSETID and CHARSETFORM are used to support NLS character sets. They are the same as the OCI attributes OCI_ATTR_CHARSET_ID and OCI_ATTR_CHARSET_FORM. For IN parameters, CHARSETID and CHARSETFORM are passed by value (by default) and are read-only. For IN OUT, OUT, and RETURN parameters, CHARSETID and CHARSETFORM are passed by reference and are read-only.

SELF is used if an object member function is implemented as a callout instead of a PL/SQL routine.

When moving data between PL/SQL and C, each PL/SQL datatype maps to an "external datatype," identified by a PL/SQL keyword, which in turn maps to an allowed set of C types:

PL/SQL types ← → External datatypes ← → C types

PL/SQL includes a special set of keywords to use as the external datatype in the PARAMETERS clause. In some cases, the external datatypes have the same name as the C types. If you pass a PL/SQL variable of type PLS_INTEGER, the corresponding default external type is INT, which maps to an int in C. But Oracle's VARCHAR2 uses the STRING external datatype, which normally maps to a char * in C.

The following table lists all the possible datatype conversions supported by Oracle's PL/SQL-to-C interface. Note that the allowable conversions depend on both the datatype and the mode of the PL/SQL formal parameter. Default mappings are shown in bold (if ambiguous).

| | | C datatypes corresponding to PL/SQL parameters that are... | |
Datatype of PL/SQL parameter	PL/SQL keyword identifying external type	IN or function return values	IN OUT, OUT, or any parameter designated as being passed BY REFERENCE
Long integer family: BINARY_ INTEGER, BOOLEAN, PLS_INTEGER	**INT**, UNSIGNED INT, CHAR, UNSIGNED CHAR, SHORT, UNSIGNED SHORT, LONG, UNSIGNED LONG, SB1, UB1, SB2, UB2, SB4, UB4, SIZE_T	**int**, unsigned int, char, unsigned char, short, unsigned short, long, unsigned long, sb1, ub1, sb2, ub2, sb4, ub4, size_t	Same list of types as at left, but use a pointer (e.g., the default is int * rather than int)

Datatype of PL/SQL parameter	PL/SQL keyword identifying external type	C datatypes corresponding to PL/SQL parameters that are...	
		IN or function return values	IN OUT, OUT, or any parameter designated as being passed BY REFERENCE
Short integer family: NATURAL, NATURALN, POSITIVE, POSITIVEN, SIGNTYPE	Same as above, except default is UNSIGNED INT	Same as above, except default is unsigned int	Same as above, except default is unsigned int *
Character family: VARCHAR2, CHAR, NCHAR, LONG, NVARCHAR2, VARCHAR, CHARACTER, ROWID	**STRING**, OCISTRING	**char ***, OCIString *	**char ***, OCIString *
NUMBER	OCINUMBER	OCINumber *	OCINumber *
DOUBLE PRECISION	DOUBLE	double	double *
FLOAT, REAL	FLOAT	float	float *
RAW, LONG RAW	**RAW**, OCIRAW	**unsigned char ***, OCIRaw *	**unsigned char ***, OCIRaw *
DATE	OCIDATE	OCIDate *	OCIDate *
Timestamp family: TIMESTAMP, TIMESTAMP WITH TIME ZONE, TIMESTAMP WITH LOCAL TIME ZONE	OCIDATETIME	OCIDateTime *	OCIDateTime *
INTERVAL DAY TO SECOND, INTERVAL YEAR TO MONTH	OCIINTERVAL	OCIInterval *	OCIInterval *

Datatype of PL/SQL parameter	PL/SQL keyword identifying external type	C datatypes corresponding to PL/SQL parameters that are...	
		IN or function return values	IN OUT, OUT, or any parameter designated as being passed BY REFERENCE
BFILE, BLOB, CLOB	OCILOBLOCATOR	OCILOBLOCATOR *	OCILOBLOCATOR * *
Descriptor of user-defined type (collection or object)	TDO	OCIType *	OCIType *
Value of user-defined collection	OCICOLL	OCIColl **, OCIArray **, OCITable **	OCIColl **, OCIArray **, OCITable **
Value of user-defined object	DVOID	dvoid *	dvoid * for final types; dvoid ** for nonfinal types

Java Language Integration

Java programmers can write server-side classes that invoke SQL and PL/SQL using standard JDBC or SQLJ calls. PL/SQL programmers can call server-side Java methods by writing a PL/SQL cover or *call spec* for Java using Oracle DDL.

Server-side Java in Oracle may be faster than PL/SQL for compute-intensive programs, but not as nimble for database access. PL/SQL is much more efficient for database-intensive routines because, unlike Java, it doesn't have to pay the overhead for converting SQL datatypes for use inside the stored program. Oracle programmers will want to continue to use PL/SQL for programs that perform a lot of database I/O, and use Java for the best raw computation performance.

The first step in creating a Java stored procedure (JSP) is writing or otherwise obtaining functional Java code. Having source code is not necessary, though, so you can use class libraries from third parties. The classes must, however, meet the following requirements:

- Methods published to SQL and PL/SQL must be declared static. PL/SQL has no mechanism for instantiating nonstatic Java classes.
- The classes must not issue any GUI calls (for example, to AWT) at runtime.

If you write your own JSP and it needs to connect to the database for access to tables or stored procedures, use standard JDBC and/or SQLJ calls in your code. Many JDBC and SQLJ reference materials are available to provide assistance in calling SQL or PL/SQL from Java, but be sure to review the Oracle-specific documentation that ships with your release.

Once you have the Java class in hand, either in source or *.class* file format, the next step is loading it into the database. Oracle's *loadjava* command-line utility is a convenient way to accomplish the load. Refer to Oracle's documentation for further assistance with *loadjava*.

The third step is to create a call spec for the Java method, specifying the AS LANGUAGE JAVA clause of the CREATE command. You may create a function or procedure cover as appropriate.

Finally, you may grant EXECUTE privileges on the new JSP using GRANT EXECUTE, and PL/SQL routines can now call the JSP as if it were another PL/SQL module.

Example

Let's write a simple "Hello, World" JSP that will accept an argument:

```
package oreilly.plsquick.demos;

public class Hello {
   public static String sayIt (String toWhom) {
      return "Hello, " + toWhom + "!";
   }
}
```

Saved in a file called *Hello.java*, the source code can be loaded directly into Oracle. Doing so will compile the code automatically. Here is a simple form of the *loadjava* command:

```
loadjava -user scott/tiger -oci8 oreilly/plsquick/
    demos/Hello.java
```

The *Hello.java* file follows the Java file placement convention for packages and thus exists in a subdirectory named *oreilly/plsquick/demos*.

We can fire up our favorite SQL interpreter, connect as SCOTT/TIGER, and create the call spec for the Hello.sayIt( ) method:

```
CREATE FUNCTION hello_there (to_whom IN VARCHAR2)
    RETURN VARCHAR2
    AS LANGUAGE JAVA
    NAME 'oreilly.plsquick.demos.Hello.sayIt
      (java.lang.String) return java.lang.String';
```

Now we can call our function very easily:

```
BEGIN
    DBMS_OUTPUT.PUT_LINE(hello_there('world'));
END;
```

And we get the following as the expected output:

```
Hello, world!
```

Publishing Java to PL/SQL

To write a call spec, use the AS LANGUAGE JAVA clause in a CREATE statement. The syntax for this clause is:

```
{ IS | AS } LANGUAGE JAVA
    NAME 'method_fullname [ (type_fullname,... ]
      [ RETURN type_fullname ]'
```

method_fullname is the package-qualified name of the Java class and method. It is case-sensitive and uses dots to separate parts of the package's full name. *type_fullname* is the package-qualified name of the Java datatype. Notice that a simple string, not a SQL name, follows the NAME keyword.

Type mapping follows most JDBC rules regarding the legal mapping of SQL types to Java types. Oracle extensions exist for Oracle-specific datatypes.

Most datatype mappings are relatively straightforward, but passing Oracle objects of a user-defined type is harder than one would think. Oracle provides a JPublisher tool that generates the Java required to encapsulate an Oracle object and its corresponding REF. Refer to Oracle's JPublisher documentation for guidelines on usage.

The AS LANGUAGE JAVA clause is the same regardless of whether you are using Java as a standalone JSP, the implementation of a packaged program, or the body of an object type method. For example, here is the complete syntax for creating JSPs as PL/SQL-callable functions or procedures:

```
CREATE [OR REPLACE]
{  PROCEDURE procedure_name [(param[, param]...)]
   | FUNCTION function_name [(param[, param]...)]
       RETURN sql_type
}
[AUTHID {DEFINER | CURRENT_USER}]
[PARALLEL_ENABLE]
[DETERMINISTIC]
{ IS | AS } LANGUAGE JAVA
    NAME 'method_fullname [ (type_fullname,... ]
      [ RETURN type_fullname ]'
```

When using Java as the implementation of a packaged procedure or function, Oracle allows you to place the Java call spec in either the package specification (where the call spec substitutes for the subprogram specification) or in the package body (where the call spec substitutes for the subprogram body). Similarly, when using JSPs in object type methods, the Java call spec can substitute for either the object type method specification or its body.

Note that Java functions typically map to PL/SQL functions, but Java functions declared void map to PL/SQL procedures. Also, you will quickly learn that mistakes in mapping PL/SQL parameters to Java parameters become evident only at runtime.

Data Dictionary

To learn what Java library units are available in your schema, look in the USER_OBJECTS data dictionary view where the *object_type* is like 'JAVA%'. If you see a Java class with INVALID status, it has not yet been resolved successfully. Note that the names of the Java source library units need not match the names of the classes they produce.

Regular Expressions (Oracle Database 10*g*)

As we mentioned earlier in this book, Oracle Database 10*g* supports the use of regular expressions via four new built-in functions: REGEXP_LIKE, REGEXP_INSTR, REGEXP_SUBSTR, and REGEXP_REPLACE. This section provides only a brief description of how regular expressions work; for a tutorial and quick reference, see the *Oracle Regular Expressions Pocket Reference*, by Jonathan Gennick and Peter Linsley (O'Reilly).

Metacharacters

Regular expressions are found in Unix utilities such as *grep*, *sed*, and the *ex* editor, in the Perl scripting language, and in many other tools. Regular expressions are a powerful and popular means of processing text, mainly because they use *metacharacters* to facilitate searching for strings. The metacharacters supported by Oracle are shown in the following table:

Pattern metacharacter	Description
*	Asterisk. Matches zero or more occurrences.
+	Plus sign. Matches one or more occurrences.
?	Question mark. Matches zero or one occurrence.
^	Caret. Matches beginning of line.
$	Dollar sign. Matches end of line.

Pattern metacharacter	Description
.	Period. Matches any single character.
\	Backslash. Treats the following metacharacter as a nonspecial character.
{m}	Curly braces. Matches exactly *m* times.
{m,}	Curly braces. Matches at least *m* times.
{m,n}	Curly braces. Matches at least *m* times, but no more than *n* times.
[]	Square brackets. Matches any of the characters in the square brackets.
|	Vertical bar. Alternation operator for specifying alternative matches.
()	Parentheses. Grouping expression.
\n	Backslash. Backreference expression (\1 through \9). Used in conjunction with ( ) to identify the *n*th occurrence of the backreferenced expression. (REGEXP_REPLACE allows up to 500 backreferences in *replacement_string*.)
[::]	Character class. Examples are [:digit:] for numeric digits or [:alnum:] for alphanumeric characters.
[..]	Collation element. Encloses multiple characters treated as one character (e.g., 'ch' in Spanish).
[==]	Equivalence class. Matches accented and unaccented versions of a letter.

REGEXP_LIKE

The REGEXP_LIKE function determines whether a specific column, variable, or text literal contains text matching a regular expression. It returns Boolean TRUE if the regular expression is found in the *source_string* and FALSE if the regular expression is not found. The syntax is:

    REGEXP_LIKE (source_string, pattern [,match_modifier])

source_string
  Character string to be searched.

pattern
  Regular expression pattern that Oracle tries to find in the *source_string*.

match_modifier

One or more modifiers that apply to the search; see the "Match Modifiers" section for information.

For example:

```
IF REGEXP_LIKE(phone_number,'^\(?212\)?'
THEN
    -- phone number begins with 212
    -- optionally enclosed by parentheses
    APPLY_NYC_SURCHARGE;
END IF;
```

REGEXP_INSTR

The REGEXP_INSTR function locates, by character position, an occurrence of text matching a regular expression. It returns the beginning or ending position of the regular expression within a string. The syntax is:

```
REGEXP_INSTR (source_string
    ,pattern
    [,beginning_position
    [,occurrence
    [,return_option
    [,match_modifier]]]])
```

source_string

Character string to be searched.

pattern

Regular expression pattern that Oracle tries to find in the *source_string*.

beginning_position

Character position at which to begin the search.

occurrence

Ordinal occurrence desired (1 = first, 2 = second, etc).

return_option

Either 0 for the beginning position or 1 for the ending position.

match_modifier

>   One or more modifiers that apply to the search; see the "Match Modifiers" section for information.

For example:

```
witty_saying := 'Man fears time, but time fears the
    Pyramids';
-- display the witty_saying
-- starting with the second occurence of the word 'time'
dbms_output.put_line(SUBSTR(witty_saying
                     ,REGEXP_INSTR
                         (witty_saying,'time',1,2)));
```

The output is:

```
time fears the Pyramids
```

REGEXP_SUBSTR

The REGEXP_SUBSTR function extracts text matching a regular expression from a character column, variable, or text literal. It returns as many matching substrings as it finds (which might be zero). The syntax is:

```
REGEXP_SUBSTR (source_string
    ,pattern
    [,position
    [,occurrence
    [,match_modifier]]])
```

source_string

>   Character string to be searched.

pattern

>   Regular expression pattern that Oracle tries to find in the *source_string*.

position

>   Character position at which to begin the search.

occurrence

>   Ordinal occurrence desired (1 = first, 2 = second, etc.).

match_modifier

> One or more modifiers that apply to the search; see the "Match Modifiers" section for information.

For example:

```
-- get the leading number part of the address
-- (up to a whitespace character)
street_number := REGEXP_SUBSTR(address_line1,
    '[[:digit:]]+[:space:]');
```

REGEXP_REPLACE

The REGEXP_REPLACE function replaces a regular expression with new text that you specify. Your replacement text may include backreferences to values in the regular expression. The syntax is:

```
REGEXP_REPLACE (source_string
    ,pattern
    [,replacement_string
    [,position
    [,occurrence
    [,match_modifier]]]])
```

source_string

> Character string to be searched.

pattern

> Regular expression pattern that Oracle tries to find in the *source_string*.

replacement_string

> Replacement text for *pattern*.

position

> Character position at which to begin the search.

occurrence

> Ordinal occurrence desired (0 = all occurrences, 1 = first, 2 = second, etc.).

match_modifier

> One or more modifiers that apply to the search; see the "Match Modifiers" section for information.

For example:

```
-- change the domain part of the email addresses
-- replace everything between the @ and the '.com' with
-- the new domain name
dbms_output.put_line(REGEXP_REPLACE(email_address
                    ,'@.*\.com','@new_domain.com'));
```

Match Modifiers

The *match_modifiers* available to the regular expression condition and functions are shown in the following table:

match_modifier	Description
i	Uses a case-insensitive search. The default behavior is based on NLS_SORT.
c	Uses a case-sensitive search. The default behavior is based on NLS_SORT.
n	Enables the dot metacharacter to match newlines.
m	Treats the *source_string* as multiple lines for purposes of the beginning and end-of-line metacharacters ^ and $.

Reserved Words

As we mentioned earlier in this book, the PL/SQL language recognizes certain identifiers (language keywords and identifiers from the STANDARD package) as having special meaning. You must not redefine these *reserved words* as identifiers in your programs.

We compiled the following list of reserved words by taking the list Oracle publishes in the V$RESERVED_WORDS data dictionary view and trying to declare them (as variables and/or procedures). If the declarations failed, we added the words to the list. Avoid using these words in your programs.

ACCESS	ADD	ALL	ALTER
AND	ANY	AS	ASC
AT	AUDIT	BEGIN	BETWEEN
BINARY_DOUBLE_INFINITY	BINARY_DOUBLE_NAN	BINARY_FLOAT_INFINITY	BINARY_FLOAT_NAN
BY	CASE	CHAR	CHECK
CLOSE	CLUSTER	COLUMN	COLUMNS
COMMENT	COMMIT	COMPRESS	CONNECT
CREATE	CURRENT	CURSOR	DATE
DECIMAL	DECLARE	DEFAULT	DELETE
DESC	DISTINCT	DROP	ELSE
END	EXCLUSIVE	EXISTS	FILE
FLOAT	FOR	FROM	FUNCTION
GRANT	GROUP	HAVING	IDENTIFIED
IF	IMMEDIATE	IN	INCREMENT
INDEX	INDEXES	INITIAL	INSERT
INTEGER	INTERSECT	INTO	IS
LEVEL	LIKE	LOCK	LONG
MAXEXTENTS	MINUS	MLSLABEL	MODE
MODIFY	NOAUDIT	NOCOMPRESS	NOT
NOWAIT	NULL	NUMBER	OF
OFFLINE	ON	ONLINE	OPEN
OPTION	OR	ORDER	OVERLAPS
PACKAGE	PCTFREE	PRIOR	PRIVILEGES
PROCEDURE	PUBLIC	RAW	RENAME
RESOURCE	RETURN	REVOKE	ROLLBACK
ROW	ROWID	ROWNUM	ROWS
SAVEPOINT	SELECT	SESSION	SET
SHARE	SIZE	SMALLINT	SQL
START	SUCCESSFUL	SYNONYM	SYSDATE
TABLE	THEN	TO	TRIGGER
TYPE	UID	UNION	UNIQUE
UPDATE	USE	USER	VALIDATE
VALUES	VARCHAR	VARCHAR2	VIEW
WHEN	WHENEVER	WHERE	WITH

Index

We'd like to hear your suggestions for improving our indexes. Send email to
index@oreilly.com.

Related Titles Available from O'Reilly

Oracle PL/SQL

Learning Oracle PL/SQL

Oracle PL/SQL Best Practices

Oracle PL/SQL Developer's
Workbook

Oracle PL/SQL Programming,
3nd Edition

Oracle Books for DBAs

Oracle DBA Checklists
Pocket Reference

Oracle RMAN
Pocket Reference

Unix for Oracle DBAs
Pocket Reference

Oracle SQL and SQL Plus

Mastering Oracle SQL

Oracle SQL Plus:
The Definitive Guide

Oracle SQL Tuning
Pocket Reference

Oracle SQL*Plus
Pocket Reference, *2nd Edition*

Oracle SQL:
The Essential Reference

Oracle

Building Oracle XML
Applications

Java Programming with
Oracle JDBC

Oracle Essentials:
Oracle Database 10g,
3nd Edition

Oracle in a Nutshell

Perl for Oracle DBAs

TOAD Pocket Reference

Keep in touch with O'Reilly

1. Download examples from our books

To find example files for a book, go to:
www.oreilly.com/catalog

select the book, and follow the "Examples" link.

2. Register your O'Reilly books

Register your book at *register.oreilly.com*

Why register your books? Once you've registered your O'Reilly books you can:

- Win O'Reilly books, T-shirts or discount coupons in our monthly drawing.
- Get special offers available only to registered O'Reilly customers.
- Get catalogs announcing new books (US and UK only).
- Get email notification of new editions of the O'Reilly books you own.

3. Join our email lists

Sign up to get topic-specific email announcements of new books and conferences, special offers, and O'Reilly Network technology newsletters at:
elists.oreilly.com

It's easy to customize your free elists subscription so you'll get exactly the O'Reilly news you want.

4. Get the latest news, tips, and tools
www.oreilly.com

- "Top 100 Sites on the Web"—PC Magazine
- CIO Magazine's Web Business 50 Awards

Our web site contains a library of comprehensive product information (including book excerpts and tables of contents), downloadable software, background articles, interviews with technology leaders, links to relevant sites, book cover art, and more.

5. Work for O'Reilly

Check out our web site for current employment opportunities:
jobs.oreilly.com

6. Contact us

O'Reilly & Associates
1005 Gravenstein Hwy North
Sebastopol, CA 95472 USA

TEL: 707-827-7000 or 800-998-9938
(6am to 5pm PST)

FAX: 707-829-0104

order@oreilly.com
For answers to problems regarding your order or our products.
To place a book order online, visit:
www.oreilly.com/order_new

catalog@oreilly.com
To request a copy of our latest catalog.

booktech@oreilly.com
For book content technical questions or corrections.

corporate@oreilly.com
For educational, library, government, and corporate sales.

proposals@oreilly.com
To submit new book proposals to our editors and product managers.

international@oreilly.com
For information about our international distributors or translation queries. For a list of our distributors outside of North America check out:
international.oreilly.com/distributors.html

adoption@oreilly.com
For information about academic use of O'Reilly books, visit:
academic.oreilly.com

O'REILLY®

Our books are available at most retail and online bookstores.
To order direct: 1-800-998-9938 • *order@oreilly.com* • *www.oreilly.com*
Online editions of most O'Reilly titles are available at *safari.oreilly.com*